Talk Therapy Isn't Enough

"One aspect of our core Self is courage, which author Natasha Senra-Pereira amply demonstrates in her writing. This book is informed by an absolute commitment to personal healing and a dedication to service. It turns out they are the same. What emerges naturally for the reader is the understanding that no matter who you are or what has happened to you, your core Self is undamaged and available, wanting to manifest. Shit has happened to you, and your parts have helped you cope. The author shows us how to go beyond 'coping' to transform the pain and embody who you truly are. This book is a much-needed gift at this time. Natasha, thank you for this important contribution to the field."

—DEREK SCOTT, RSW; Certified IFS Consultant;
Founder and CEO, IFSCA

Talk Therapy Isn't Enough is a vulnerable tell-all of one psychotherapist's journey to heal herself and experience wholeness. The author's account of her personal journey contains immense Dharma (universal truth applicable to all humans) that can benefit all of us. The balance of her life story and intimate sharing of her personal development and therapeutic sessions creates an exciting read that immersed me from the first page until the last. When one of us awakens, it opens the doors for us all to do the same. This book is a great way to open those doors!"

—JESSE HANSON, PhD

"This book should give hope and help to many in their struggle toward health."

—ROBERT FALCONER, co-author, *Many Minds, One Self*,
IFS teacher/consultant

"Kudos to Natasha Senra-Pereira and her groundbreaking book *Talk Therapy Isn't Enough*. From her life experiences, educational training, and personal search, she shares with the reader her journey through various modalities of personal trauma healing from the traditional to the non-traditional. This is a real story with real feelings and real challenges. It is a gutsy, sometimes raw, but always uplifting account of how relentless searching and open-mindedness can lead to wholeness and ultimate personal redemption. Natasha opens doors to trauma healing that heretofore have rarely, if ever, been employed together concerning their individual power and scope. She flings those doors wide open. Her story is one of allowing one's search for healing to be a true search . . . looking for and finding help in an open-hearted way without judgment of each process and with a willingness to use all the tools available to heal. Her result: a whole life filled with hope and love and healing. This is a must-read for all who are interested personally and/or professionally in finding authentic trauma healing."

—**JANICE HAYES,** Doctor of RoHun Therapy

"Author Natasha Senra-Periera has achieved something remarkable with *Talk Therapy Isn't Enough*. She has banished the wounded healer archetype to the outlands by sharing her story honestly and with perspicacity. The only way a person survives the upbringing she did, with heart and mind whole, is to reach deep inside and surrender to the possibility that trauma can be a powerful teacher. Through her lived example, Natasha proves that openhearted experience, a curiosity about one's edges, and, above all, a real desire to heal can yield lessons that guide a person home. Telling this truth can be dangerous. It takes bravery to describe all that happens, good and bad, on the healing path. *Talk Therapy Isn't Enough* is something altogether new, and it offers a perspective on healing that is groundbreaking—welcome medicine for our times and our world."

—**MATT FLUGGER,** Executive Producer, *The Divine Field*

"After reading *Talk Therapy Isn't Enough*, my heart is full, and a smile plays on my lips. I have laughed, I have cried, and I have seen myself in her words and story. This book is an act of good medicine. I recommend it, especially for therapists who long for permission to speak more fully of their own spiritual and mystical experiences, and as inspiration for anyone to see 'symptoms' as calls to follow your heart, mind, body, and soul wherever is needed to find healing."

—**DR. RISA ADAMS,** MA, MD, CCRP, Certified IFS Consultant

TALK THERAPY ISN'T ENOUGH

A Psychotherapist's Personal Transformation
Through NEUROSCIENCE,
PSYCHEDELICS, and SPIRITUALITY

Natasha Senra-Pereira MSW, RSW, RP

modern wisdom
PRESS

Modern Wisdom Press
Boulder, Colorado, USA
www.modernwisdompress.com
Copyright © Natasha Senra-Pereira, 2022

Published 2022

Cover Design: Melinda Martin
Cover photo courtesy of author
Author Photo: Shelagh Howard

DISCLAIMER

Neither the author nor the publisher assumes any responsibility for errors, omissions, or contrary interpretations of the subject matter within.

MEDICAL DISCLAIMER

The information in this book is a result of years of practical experience by the author. This information is not intended as a substitute for the advice provided by your physician or other healthcare professional. Do not use the information in this book for diagnosing or treating a health problem or disease, or prescribing medication or other treatment.

To my mother, for her resilience and courage and unconditional love for my boys.

And to my boys—you are my sunshine, you'll never know how much I love you.

Contents

Talk Therapy Isn't Enough!

When my dear friend and colleague, Natasha, told me she was writing a book to demonstrate that talk therapy isn't enough, I shouted, "Finally! Halleluiah! It's about time!"

I began seeing how talk therapy wasn't enough in the early 1980s while watching the rise of Cognitive Behavioral Therapy. There is nothing wrong with CBT and other behavioral modalities, as they can help you get from today until tomorrow. They help you cope. My interest has long been in going beyond coping to transformation and thriving: Living a life of presence, meaningful connections, and deep satisfaction.

I was a renegade therapist as I discovered the effects of our earliest experiences and how working with the whole body took clients further faster. In 1982 I became the founding Academic Dean of Pacifica Graduate Institute, where we trained clinical psychology graduate students in whole-body learning and Jungian or imaginal therapy. In 2000 my husband, Ken Bruer, and I founded a college offering the first doctoral degrees in somatic psychology and the first masters' and doctoral degrees in prenatal and perinatal psychology. Our professors were pioneers. Stanislav Grof, MD, PhD, brought transpersonal psychology and non-ordinary states of consciousness. Bruce H. Lipton, PhD, brought epigenetics. Rollin McCraty, PhD, of the HeartMath Institute, brought heart coherence. Allan N. Schore, PhD, brought attachment and neuroscience. Peter A. Levine, PhD, brought new methods of working with trauma. Daniel Siegel, MD, PhD, supported us with his interpersonal neurobiology. Many of our professors were teaching their research which demonstrated, basically, talk therapy isn't enough. We need to incorporate every aspect of our being, not just our thinking and behavior.

I remember several years ago when Natasha showed up as a client at one of our Ryzio retreats in Arizona. Having worked with thousands of therapists internationally for decades, Natasha seemed different. Although she was timid at first, I was attracted to her authentic presence, incredible commitment to her own healing, deep dedication to her boys, and determination to be the best possible therapist for her clients. She was willing to slow down, look deeply within and discover her gifts. It has been very meaningful to me that we have stayed in touch over the years as she sent her clients to us at Ryzio. And as she engaged fully in our training to become a Certified Ryzio Coach, I could see her growing personally and professionally. She is an excellent coach and therapist and a rare treasure.

Traversing the path of the Heroic Journey, Natasha leads us through inspiring and heart-breaking stories—stories that can mirror your own path and encourage you to keep going. I found myself in tears as I turned some of the pages, and at other times, in great suspense, not being able to put the book down. Here you will experience the dynamics of love and loss, presence and absence, and parental interactions moving between deep love and caring and unconscious, unconscionable abuse.

Natasha is authentic and vulnerable through these stories, bearing her soul and showing us the way. You can feel her resilience as she keeps going. She never takes no for an answer. Somehow, the little girl who learned to take care of everyone else begins to find her own voice and path to strength, wholeness, forgiveness, and love. She traces her years of talk therapy from teen to adult, uncovering how it never quite measured up or did what it was supposed to do.

In this journey of listening to her intuition and trying different therapies and healing modalities, she walks us through what is possible. She looks at therapy from the inside out: what works and why. And she invites us to look inward and be curious.

We see both a personal and professional view of several powerful and proven modalities that go beyond talking and thinking and into shifting old belief structures that hinder us from experiencing love and connection. We witness what's possible when we consider our earliest experiences and apply holistic, body-oriented therapies.

Natasha's raw and riveting narrative shows a door beginning to open to possibilities using plant medicine and psychedelics—currently a leading edge of psychotherapy and healing. We are now learning to safely access the power of non-ordinary states of consciousness to transform our lives safely and quickly. This is done with great support through preparation and integration.

The stories in *Talk Therapy Isn't Enough* show how it's possible to release the burden of your history and the effects of trauma. You will witness the dissolving of pain and suffering, helplessness and loss of self, and the experience of gratitude, personal power, and joy. This book shows us how we can go beyond talk therapy to experiencing our gifts and sharing them with others. We can genuinely receive and live in a place of wholeness and love.

I invite you to step in and experience what's possible when you go beyond talk therapy!

—**Marti Glenn**, PhD
Chief Clinical Officer, Ryzio Institute
www.ryzio.com
Santa Barbara, California

Introduction

I have been called an impatient therapist. I am impatient about many things. As someone who has been a social worker and psychotherapist for almost twenty years, I have found much to be impatient about. I worked with various populations at the largest mental health hospital in Canada and was well trained in popular modalities such as Cognitive Behavioral Therapy, Dialectical Behavior Therapy, Emotion Focused Therapy, Narrative Therapy, and many other forms of talk therapy. Over time, I became impatient with how little movement my clients were making, and it seemed that our vast hospital resources were going to treating symptoms rather than causes.

One pivotal day, I was working on a crisis unit, when a patient came in—a tall and elegant man in his fifties diagnosed with everything under the sun. He had been using mental health emergency rooms for a decade, looking for help when his shadows and demons tormented him. He was an entrepreneur who had worked hard to overcome unimaginable life experiences in childhood and adolescence. When these unprocessed traumas came for him, he feared for himself and his family and went to emergency rooms, having exhausted therapy groups and treatment.

As I read over his chart, I could see the courage and incredible resilience of this man. But when I listened to the staff go over his chart, my impatience partnered with my outrage. The team didn't use his name. They didn't read the words in his chart. Instead, they hastily pushed his file to me for discharge.

To them, he was taking up space. There were no more medications to try, and he had done all the manualized groups and worksheets we could offer. There were no more resources. I have worked on teams with psychologists, psychiatrists, pharmacists, recreational therapists, occupational therapists, dieticians, art therapists, and endless admin staff. Yet, I always hear we have no resources.

I didn't ask questions. I accepted the answer. Systems are complex, and resources scarce. But that day, with this man, my impatience woke me up. It said to me, "Of course, there are no beds; of course, the staff is apathetic. But it's not because we don't have resources. It's because we pour our resources like water into the sand."

I knew this man did not need more coping skills; he needed healing. But we didn't do that in the system, and there was nowhere to send him. So that day, all I could offer him was respect and kindness. I was not going to sleepwalk and give lazy answers when sending him away; I was going to be awake.

I told him we had nothing for him, not because of him, but because of us. I gave him the same handouts he was given last time. I looked him in the eye. I softened the tone of my voice and apologized for not being able to deliver what he deserved. He lowered his head and gave me a small smile. He thanked me for being kind and said that he knew there was nothing for him but that my kindness helped. He walked away, looking at me and saying, "You're one of us."

I began to cry. He was right; I was one of "us." I, too, had been doing the worksheets, the handouts of coping strategies, and seeing the same talk therapist for sixteen years. Every week I sat in his office rehearsing the painful stories of my chaotic upbringing and developing insight into how I was replicating similar patterns in the present. But no amount of insight mattered; the patterns remained. I was still rageful, distrustful, and anxious.

And then, my marriage ended, I quit therapy and embarked on a journey that would lead to true healing and transformation, one that would be guided by therapists who specialized in neuroscience modalities like Eye Movement Desensitization and Reprocessing (EMDR) and somatic explorations and Internal Family Systems (IFS) work. I also moved beyond modalities of the Western world and into the traditions of psychedelics (psilocybin) and the metaphysical and spiritual (yoga, meditation, quantum physics). These processes moved me out of unconsciously living my life in chaos, conditioned in my childhood, into creating my life from adult wisdom and finding a depth of consciousness that brought me inner freedom, peace, and joy.

As I was going through the processes myself, I also brought these new learnings into my private practice with individual clients and shared them with friends and colleagues. I watched the same incredible, life-changing transformations in them that I experienced.

Over time, I realized I had an extraordinary blueprint for healing based on the understanding that traumas are not the *events* in our lives but rather the *impact* of those events on our internal systems. We do ourselves a disservice by understanding our present suffering as *mental health issues* and *symptoms* instead of understanding what we are being called to release: depression (unprocessed pain), anxiety (unprocessed fear), and codependency (unmet developmental needs). And we do a disservice to our loved ones and family members by holding them in positions of shame and blame when we all operate out of trauma, unconsciously hurting each other as we hurt ourselves.

After years of supporting clients in my private practice with this blueprint, I am bringing the following pages to you. You will see that my healing journey has not been a linear path—because there is no one path. What I offer here is a series of paths to healing. In the following pages, I invite you to follow me in both my training and my experience as a client. I hope that sharing my process offers you a deep understanding of what each modality provides, along with the ongoing importance of integration. Not all of these processes will apply to you, nor will you likely need them all. I required many different modalities to heal from suffering to experience first-hand the cycle of pain and triumphs (and pain again) that comprise this path of expansion and contraction.

My hope is that this book will be of use to you individually and to all of us as a collective as we move out of a culture of blame and victimhood and turn inward. May it help us empower ourselves to accept how we co-create the world we live in and take responsibility for the lives we lead. I hope that sharing all of me will lead to healing for some parts of you.

PART I

FATE

CHAPTER I

The Ordinary World

Adam's office was at Avenue Road and Eglinton, and he charged double what my last therapist charged. I was desperate enough that I would come up to this expensive part of town and pay this kind of money. I sat in his beautiful waiting room with its organic tea station in the corner, the smell of Palo Santo and chanting music in the background. When he came out to greet me, he seemed almost to float across the room, the sunlight streaming in behind him as a serene gaze was directed my way.

"Natasha," he said kindly. He pronounced it "Naw-Tosh-A," which I generally hated but it seemed to work coming from him. Adam's long hair was perfectly styled to appear shaggy and messy, and his bangs draped over his pretty blue eyes. He had a perfectly coiffed beard and was dressed in an expensive-looking outfit with casual linen pants and a shirt unbuttoned to show a broad, tanned chest and a shark's tooth necklace nestled in golden chest hair. Also, he was barefoot. Adam was a therapist with a PhD and a speciality in neuroscience, but he seemed like some kind of new age hippie.

He invited me into his shag-carpeted office and told me he had moved a few years ago from California to Toronto, where he and his wife had recently welcomed their infant son. He was calm and easygoing, and I could tell he was also smart. As I began to talk about why I was looking for a new therapist, I surprised myself by bursting into tears. Adam waited quietly for me to contain myself and gave me the frame of his practice. It was primarily somatic, he said, a new model for healing that differed greatly from the one I had been trained in.

He explained that our past trauma is stored in the body, and the human nervous system is constantly activated by external situations and events in our present-day life. Put simply, when I felt rage at the Starbucks barista for getting my coffee order wrong, that emotion was most likely a triggered somatic (bodily) response, stored from my childhood, about chronically being overlooked and disregarded in my family. I nodded although a part of me was skeptical. But I was out of options. So, I sat on the couch and waited to have him tell me how to put my life together.

Instead, Adam asked if it would be okay for me to close my eyes and breathe, feeling into my body. I agreed, but as I slowly inhaled, I became aware that I couldn't do what he was asking. My chest felt tight, my breaths shallow. Another wave of tears came, except this time they were more like sobs as the reality of my current life circumstances flooded over me. Adam asked if he could approach me and I nodded with my head in my hands, eyes shut tightly. I felt him come over to the couch and wrap what felt like a rope around me, tightly binding my arms to my sides. When I was constricted to the point where my shallow breathing was due to external pressure, Adam asked if the sensation was okay, if I could still breathe. I nodded, the sobs quieting to tears rolling down my cheeks.

Adam was sitting next to me then, his presence gentle, his voice nurturing. He said, "Can you see yourself, bound like this, holding all this pain? Look down with your Eagle Eyes. What do you see?" To my surprise I could see. I saw a young woman trying hard to be so good and so pure and so loving. I saw a woman terrified by all of the happenings of her life, a woman who put one foot in front of the other every day, struggling to take care of people: her kids, her husband, her parents, clients, the bus driver, everyone. This was a woman who worked desperately hard to make sure all those around her were okay. This poor woman was tiny, vulnerable, and scared. All these words and descriptions tumbled out of my mouth to Adam, and from my Eagle Eyes, I watched my body shrink even smaller, my head hanging so limply it almost touched my knees with the weight and exhaustion of years of trying to get through. I just wept.

Then suddenly, Adam yanked me up hard by the blanket that bound me. With my eyes still instinctively closed, he pulled me around the room, helpless and tied up. His voice changed, and he taunted, "Get up, little social worker, get up and keep taking care of everyone. Move, get moving, there's more to do," he said as he jerked me from side to side. I didn't fight it, couldn't; I had nothing left. The yanking continued for only a few moments, but I got it. I felt in my body how I lacked the compassion and softness toward myself that I needed. Adam led me back to the couch and unwound the blanket. I opened my eyes and looked at him. There seemed to be pain in his gaze. I saw that it hurt him to witness my suffering.

I quietly thanked him. He nodded. As I was gathering my things, he suggested we meet regularly, if possible, because I had a lot of work to do. I agreed. And I hadn't yet mentioned a word about my family, my story.

––––––

I married Paul when I was twenty-eight. We bought and renovated our first home and had our son Jesse when I was thirty and our second son, Abe, when I was thirty-three. I did everything I was supposed to do, and I found myself lost, my marriage collapsing, by the time I was thirty-seven.

Paul and I could be a loving couple, making each other laugh, and we were committed to building a better family for ourselves than the ones we were born into. He was devoted to me, and I nurtured and cared for him with all of my being. However, we could also be explosive toward each other, replicating many of the past wounds we hoped we'd escaped in adulthood, when we were free to make our own choices. These episodes were ugly and usually ended with me screaming threats and pushing him out the door. Regardless, we always seemed to get back on track. I would forgive Paul for what I viewed as his reckless, impulsive behavior, and he saw past my controlling and angry outbursts. We were able to look beyond our problems and feel into the gentle and sensitive people we were at our core. As a clinical social worker and therapist, I explained away our unhealthy dynamics, understanding that my chaotic childhood and his upbringing had a lot to do with how we reacted in the world and to it.

Over the years, our problems seemed to escalate, and the more he pushed, the more I pulled. The issues didn't get better, but there was less energy to battle about them as we grew exhausted by the fighting and let more slide, distracted by life and parenthood. We went to individual and couples counseling, patching up our relationship and enjoying each other for months at a time—until the old wounds resurfaced. Paul, who loved being a father, was committed to our children—for which I was grateful—but his fierce protectiveness of them against my family was an ongoing issue in our marriage. In the end, the container we built at twenty-four years old, when we first met, didn't hold the frustrated, restless, and angry me who was resentful toward her roles as wife and mother. Even though I desperately loved my husband and children, I didn't know how to be in that container any longer, and our fights were escalating. The dynamic between us began to feel a lot like the one I had in my family growing up—*I will try to be anything you need me to be and yet I can't survive being the way you need me to be.*

Origins

My family of origin had always been tumultuous, which would have been easier to accept if they weren't also incredibly loving, compassionate, and generous people. The insidious polarization of my family's presentation manifested a similar complexity and polarization in me and my siblings. We children learned to survive by understanding our parents and their different personalities and behaving as they did. Paul initially adapted well to the clan because they were likable, with good hearts. But he, too, got caught up in their turmoil when they seemed to flip a switch and operate from a place of control and cruelty. Things changed permanently for him with the birth of our first son.

Jesse had been born three weeks early, jaundiced, and wouldn't feed. My engorged breasts ached, and he wouldn't latch or take a bottle. We were told we'd be in the hospital for a few days. He needed light treatment for the jaundice and support with feeding from a little tube attached to my finger that he was able to suck on. As new parents, Paul and I were exhausted, disoriented, and scared for our little guy. He had only been in the world a few hours when Paul called our families, delivering the news that Jesse was born, and we were all doing fine but needed some time to rest, recover, and speak to the doctors. Paul explained he would call later in the day when we were ready for visitors.

Ignoring our request, Mom burst through the hospital doors within the hour. Beaming from ear to ear, she sang in a loud voice, "Where's my grandson?" as she threw her oversized purse on the bed. She rested it on my feet before pulling out a Corona and a meat sandwich wrapped in tin foil from the Portuguese butcher, which she thrust into Paul's hand. It was 8:30 in the morning. She didn't acknowledge me at all. Excited to see Jesse, she went over to his incubator and began tapping on the glass as if he were a fish, trying to get his attention. He was sleeping and blindfolded with a little mask to protect his still-forming eyes from the bright treatment light. I watched this woman hop from foot to foot as she squealed, "Hello, hello! Here I am! Your grandmother!" Paul just stood there with the beer in his hand, looking at my mother in shock.

I wasn't surprised. I knew that asking for privacy wouldn't work. I knew that asking for what I needed was futile. Right at that moment, the doctor came in and introduced herself before she kindly and patiently answered the questions I uttered in nervous, just-delivered-a-baby exhaustion. As the doctor examined my sore breasts, she spoke to me about finger feeding. My mother, still tapping the incubator, waved dismissively and said, "This breastfeeding is nonsense. I didn't with you and you're fine."

That was it for Paul. He politely, yet firmly, told my mother this was a stressful time, and we needed rest and a chance to talk to the doctors privately. If she could please give us some space, we'd call her later in the day when it was time for visitors.

I held my breath, stunned at his boldness. The light drained from my mother's eyes, and a cold, steely expression crossed over her face. She picked up her purse, lighter without the meat sandwiches and beer, and walked out. A few hours later, when Jesse had begun feeding through the tube and I had an hour of sleep, I called my family to talk about Jesse and how we were doing. My parents wouldn't take my calls and neither would my younger sister and brother. I could only reach their voicemails. I knew it was deliberate. I had been punished this way by them many times before.

When I finally got my father on the phone, he told me how I had offended my mother, that I was being controlling, and how dare I keep the family from the baby. I began sobbing, feeling ashamed of my behavior, as well as scared and overwhelmed by the huge task ahead of me—keeping Jesse alive. For Paul, the image of me in the corner of the hospital room in tears, pleading into the phone to my father, and apologizing for asking my mother to leave, soured him on my parents. My mother's behavior in the next few weeks further propelled Paul to begin dismantling our relationship with them.

After we brought Jesse home, my mother, still deeply offended, set out to punish me for the next few weeks by visiting me but forbidding my siblings and father from answering my calls. I was properly shamed and put in my place by my family, and like a good daughter I shut my mouth and let her dominate every situation. When friends would come over to see Jesse, my mother would start vacuuming under their feet to disrupt the visit. My friends would look at me confused, remembering my mother clad in a Diana Ross wig and stilettos, dressed up and lip syncing "I'll Be There" at my baby shower, and clearly wondered if that charismatic and charming woman was the same one yanking the baby from their arms and insisting he needed to nap.

That first month of Jesse's life was miserable, and Paul struggled the most. He and my mother engaged in an absurd dance where he would put Jesse down for a nap in the coolest corner of the house, this being an unusually hot September, only to have my mother come right behind him and pour three wool blankets over the sleeping baby. Paul had read all the baby books and was up to date on the surgeon general's latest information, and would quickly take off the blankets and attempt to educate my mother on the dangers of sudden infant death syndrome (SIDS) and overheating. My mother would get that familiar glazed look over her face and nod at him, stepping back. I would watch as Paul, feeling satisfied that he got through to her, walked away triumphantly, only to have my mother tuck the blankets around Jesse's warm body again as soon as he turned his back, SIDS be damned.

It all came to a head one day when I was finally able to have a nice, long, steamy shower. I was settling into that much-needed solitude when I heard screaming from the front door. I flung a towel over myself and ran downstairs, worried the house was on fire. I wished it had been. Instead, I saw my 5'1" mother shaking and thrusting her finger in Paul's face. Paul looked over at me, and I could see by his expression that this was the last straw for him. I watched from the landing as my mother said, "You listen to me, Paul. You may be a first-time father, but I'm a first-time grandmother and nobody is going to have me make an appointment to see my grandson." *Oh*, I thought. *He had asked her to call before she came: big mistake.*

I calmed my mother and sent her on her way, then headed upstairs to find Paul singing to Jesse. I knelt next to them, crying softly and saying I was exhausted. Paul said that I was too used to punishment and shame from my family, and he would take the lead in making decisions for us. I nodded, miserable. I couldn't balance everyone's needs anymore.

Quitting

My parents and I were never the same after Jesse's birth, and for that, I was relieved but also profoundly sad. Meanwhile, Paul and I redoubled our efforts to shape a life around our children, a family experience that dodged the toxicity of our own upbringings. I had been a therapist at Canada's largest mental health hospital for over a decade and I loved the work and the clients, but I hated the organizational politics and navigating the egos of the psychiatrists and my colleagues. Each time I returned from a maternity leave, my role would change, further reducing direct contact with clients and increasing my time on administrative duties and triaging clients toward group education and medication consultations. After Abe was born, I was happy to go to work but miserable about the tasks I was required to perform.

My boss viewed me as a pain in the ass, observing that I was the first one to speak up in meetings about patients' rights and to remind the other clinicians these were human beings with feelings and needs, not just walking, talking symptoms. My patients and the administrative staff loved me, but the doctors and management team wanted me out of their hair. After my maternity leave with Abe, I came back to my office to find two gigantic computer screens, a headset, and instructions to triage clients over the phone for single-session assessments with psychiatry. No longer would I meet with patients face-to-face to provide support. I was back at work only a few weeks when Paul, tired of my complaints, suggested that if I hated it so much, I should quit, start my own private practice, and do things my way. He was stressed out and busy with his own career, and the weight of raising two kids by ourselves with no external family support was pushing us past our breaking point as a couple. I was miserable and exhausted at home and miserable and restless at work. The more I sat at my desk with my headset and screens instead of a human being in front of me, the more my mind would wander and dream about forging my own career path. Maybe that would balance my unhappiness at home. Each day at work, I gritted my teeth in my new mainly administrative role until I'd had enough and went home to plan for my new private practice and future.

The next day I told my boss that I was giving my two weeks' notice. She smiled up at me and said she wished me well. I blinked. *What? That's it?* And then I realized—they needed me gone. I had been standing in the way of their agenda for too long. I was equipped to make something happen on my own even if I didn't know what that was yet.

Selfish

Along with choosing my own practice and devoting my time and energy to something other than my husband and children came guilt for honoring my own needs. It was automatic, the weight I felt when I didn't adapt to the demands of my family. And the guilt wasn't just from me; it felt like it was from Paul too. This angered me, as I felt stifled and forced into exclusive roles as wife and mother, and our fights began escalating to dangerous levels of toxicity. In childhood I had a strong sense of right and wrong that didn't align with my mother's agendas, and that continued to play out at work, with Paul, and with anyone I felt was trying to control me. However, there was always a wave of shame and self-judgment when I chose myself. The perception that I was being selfish came crashing up to the surface. I had been working on not being selfish my entire life, learning at a young age from my mother I possessed that terrible personality trait. In those early days, my younger sister worked at soothing and managing my mother. I spent most of my time out of the house, busy with after-school sports and babysitting jobs, which provided me some respite from my mom. I was grateful for the other adults in my life—the teachers at school, other kids' parents—who provided me with some encouragement, praise, and positive attention as my mother's depression and rages worsened and become more unpredictable. But I couldn't fully escape her, as she seemed to save up her more intense fury for me. She was always finding ways to trap me in cars, offering me rides to friends' houses to unleash torrents of shame and judgment at me. When she had me buckled in and on the road, she would begin telling me all the things wrong with me and how I make those around me miserable. Although I could sense the anger and wildness in her, during these car rides, she delivered her abuse with the calmness of a queen, telling me she was doing it "for your own good."

She would say, "You know, Natasha, I've been listening to the way you talk on the phone with your friends. I'm telling you this to help you, but you are selfish with your friends, always talking about yourself. If you aren't more careful no one will want to be around you, because people don't like others who only care about themselves. I've seen you do that with your sister. You aren't a nice person."

As I got older, she would make it about my appearance or how I was interacting with boys, telling me to be careful that others didn't think of me as a "slut" because I spent my time rollerblading around the city with the group of neighborhood boys I had grown up with. I was a tomboy and a better skater than most of them, but my mother made sure to let me know that how I was being perceived by others was "loose." I stopped accepting invitations to go for the nightly neighborhood skates.

So here I was, at the crossroads, choosing whether to focus on myself and my career or on the needs of my young family. I didn't know if this meant I was truly being selfish or taking control of my life and following what felt right for me. It was confusing. All I knew was that I was stepping into unfamiliar territory of not having a plan going forward, but knowing I couldn't stay where I was.

CHAPTER II

Answering the Call

My body and I have always had a complex relationship. We haven't had a relationship so much as my head tells it what to do, and my loyal, strong, and devoted body shape-shifts itself to comply. The first time I remember being able to control my body was when I was seven years old and went with my mother's whole extended family to the Centre Island theme park. My mother was acting strangely all day, including ushering me away from the group to go on a ride even though she generally stayed away from them due to her extreme motion sickness. She couldn't seem to get me to the rollercoasters quickly enough, and on one particular ride, she scrambled to hoist herself next to me, jumping backward and landing on my outstretched arm. I cried out as her body weight snapped the bone, but I quickly quieted myself and ignored the white-hot pain as she looked at me harshly and shushed me, telling me to stop crying and contain myself. Even though I was young, I could see how scared she was, afraid that she was going to get in trouble for hurting me even though it was an accident. It was only when my father saw me walking toward him with a plastered smile on my face and my broken arm hanging uselessly from my shoulder that I got some medical attention and a cast put on me at the hospital.

All these years later, my body was no longer willing to morph according to my mind's requirements. The dynamic between me and Paul was worsening, and my body was shutting down, refusing to let me ignore the tensions and go back to playing wife and mother. It wouldn't let me embrace my husband, it recoiled at the idea of sleeping in our bed, and it rejected standing in circles with other mothers talking about our children's potential allergies. No amount of coaxing from my head would convince it to relax and go along with the life I had worked so hard to build.

Talk Therapy

I was a walking battlefield. Whenever I thought about the possibility of divorce, my mind would go to all the beautiful things about Paul and married life with the kids, and when I thought about staying, my body recoiled. I was trapped between two different parts of me. The part that wanted to stay kept reminding me of the security and safety of my married life, regardless of the chaotic dynamic between Paul and me. Simultaneously, my body seemed to reject being at the house. I was also scared of the unknown, unsure where I would live and what I would do for money if I did leave. I had just started my own business and no longer had the security of a nine-to-five job with benefits and a pension. Reading about the Toronto housing market terrified me, and I knew I could never afford to buy our home from Paul. On and on my thoughts would race, considering all the options and solutions. But as time went on, I could feel my body refusing to inhabit what was my old life. It didn't seem to matter how much my mind tried to convince me to stay with Paul; my body issued a NO loudly, from deep within.

I had been working with the same therapist since I was twenty years old. He had been my mother's therapist for about ten years, and I agreed to join her for a session, hoping it could help our complicated relationship. For all my anger and resentment toward my mom, I also loved her deeply and felt protective of her and all she had endured in her life. When my mother was stable, she was a deeply generous, kind, and loving person who devoted herself to the family's well-being. The problem was you never knew which mother you were going to get: the stable one or the unstable one. Unfortunately, on the day of our joint therapy session, I realized too late which mother had walked me into the office. When we sat down, the therapist asked, "Why are we here today?" and my mother exhaled loudly and said, "We're here today because Natasha has been a great disappointment to me." My mother then began to list all the ways I had fallen short of her expectations. The therapist watched me watch my mother and said, "Are you going to sit there and let her talk about you this way?" My mother and I looked at each other and laughed, confused about what he was talking about.

At the end of the session, he asked my mother to wait in the waiting room and then turned to me. "The dynamic between your mother and you is troubling," he said, "and I estimate it has been lifelong. If you're interested, I'd be open to working with you with one caveat: Your family cannot pay for your therapy. If they do, they can always pull it and manipulate you with it." It was true. I had been on my own navigating my family. I said yes and began to pay him all I could afford, about a third of what he charged, and saw him weekly on and off for sixteen years.

When Paul and I got married, he became our couples therapist, and anytime we would have an argument Paul would say, "I think you need to make an appointment for yourself," letting me know I needed to regulate myself and get my therapist to help me get back on track. My friend Melissa had seen this same therapist (several of my friends saw him on account of my referrals) and didn't appreciate some of his old-school perspectives on divorce and sex. That is what Melissa had begun working on after she had ended her marriage and started looking to date. I ignored a lot of her opinions on him as he was the only person in my life who seemed calm and grounded and as if he cared about me. Throughout my work with him in my early twenties, he had supported me in navigating my family and mirroring for me that I was not the difficult daughter my parents insisted I was, but that instead I was a person who wanted healthier boundaries and relationships that were threatening to the codependent and dysfunctional dynamics. Unfortunately, the triad of him, me, and Paul didn't work well because Paul was sitting there talking about how challenging and selfish I was; this time, my therapist was trying to rescue him.

I went to see him on my own before Paul joined for a couples session. I told the therapist about my body's refusal to get in the bed and its rejection of my life. My therapist, the person I trusted more than anyone in the world, looked at me in that moment and said, "You have to get back in the bed." My body began rejecting my therapist.

The End Before the Beginning

My body was winning. For three months it had insisted that I sleep alone in the basement. Even though my emotions and my behavior continued the dysfunctional patterns with Paul, my body refused to play along. It was time for a separation. After I told Paul, I had to tell the kids.

Before we talked to Jesse about the separation, I hung a big piece of bristol board on the wall and outlined the 2-2-3 day schedule I had borrowed from my girlfriends' separation, in which we switched off every two days and then alternated weekends for a three-day stretch, color-coding when I would be at the house with the boys and when Paul would be. Then I gathered myself up and with confidence and gentleness told the kids that Mommy and Daddy wouldn't be living in the house together at the same time. I explained we loved each other and Jesse and Abe, but we were going to take turns being with them. They took it well. Afterward, I completely fell apart.

The first person I told was my friend Rita, who had always looked up to me and Paul for how we persevered and kept working on our relationship. Rita had witnessed the love Paul and I had for each other and all the work we had done in therapy over the years. Shocked to hear about the separation, she insisted this was a blip, and we'd be fine, getting through it as we always had. I shook my head. As I started to tell her a little about the events that led up to this, my voice caught in my throat. Rita quickly pulled back her chair and put her hands up and said, "Don't worry. I won't touch you." I had forgotten how well I had trained my friends to give me space if I became emotional. Crying in front of them only seemed to happen if I'd been drinking, which wasn't often. On rare occasions, I would have one more drink than I should have and wind up sitting around a table with friends and sharing some of the deep, dark feelings I had about myself and some of my childhood experiences. If any of them tried to comfort me, I would push them away and leave immediately. I didn't want to be hugged, and I didn't want to be seen.

In private, I would sit before the long mirror that hung inside my closet, chain-smoking as I safely shared all the secrets of my family and my life, reassuring myself and telling myself to go to bed. I knew it was strange, but sitting in front of mirrors and soothing myself was a habit I had developed when I was young. The person in the mirror was kind, needed nothing from me, and was always there to listen for however long I needed to talk. Having Rita pull away right then, when I was in need, reminded me of how much I had lived my life on my own, surrounded by people yet alone in the dark.

A Quiet Place

I found an apartment. It was the top two stories of a three-story home in the Annex neighborhood at Bloor and Bathurst. The online photos indicated it had wood beams, exposed brick, and a loft-style bedroom. I had scheduled the visit around my clients so I looked nice and hoped my professional look would instill some confidence in the owner about renting me the space. I hit the bell and waited. No answer. I hit it again, and after a moment, I heard some movement in the house. I spotted feet through the window of the door, and then legs that were attached to the most beautiful man I had ever seen. Not only was he the most beautiful man I had ever seen, but he was also the most beautiful creature I had ever *felt*. It was strange that I could *feel* him, but I could.

The door opened and I looked up into calm, deep brown eyes "Hi. Natasha?"

I stared. This man was tall, perhaps just over six feet, and those gentle eyes were big and wide set, accompanied by a strong and large nose and thick lips with perfectly white teeth. He had a rugged, short beard, the perfect length that didn't seem groomed or planned, just natural. Dark, thick, wavy hair curled at his temples and down his neck, also in a natural way, as he seemed to have no particular care for grooming. His body was long, lean, and muscular, as if he was active but not at the gym.

"You must be James," I said, pulling myself together. He nodded and invited me in. I was nervous, wanting this to be the apartment, so at least I had a plan. As I followed James up the stairs, I listened to myself spilling out all the personal details of my life and why I needed the apartment. I couldn't believe how much I was telling this stranger. Scanning the space, I felt myself slow down and become aware of how safe and comfortable I felt there with the apartment's natural light and big, airy rooms. James went into the kitchen and fiddled with a bright yellow kettle to make us tea as I surveyed his incredible meticulousness. And then it hit me: *He's gay*, a realization that surprised and relaxed me, and likewise brought up shame that I was so attracted to him when I should be focusing on the mess of my life. Another few minutes of my crazy talking and some shared laughs with James, and it was time to go. He said other people would be viewing the space but he'd let me know in a few days.

Trauma Begets Trauma

After the separation, I started seeing my mother more. Growing up, when Mom was in one of her dark spells, she would tell me I caused her emotional state. I never knew what I was doing wrong, but she would often snap, "You just wake up trying to see how you can ruin my day," or "Why do you always need to make everything so challenging?" It was true that I often refused to play along in whatever drama she was actively creating. My sister did a much better job of being agreeable and knew how to stay out of my mother's way. For whatever reason, I didn't, instead calling out my mother's actions that didn't make sense to me.

My mother always seemed either to be running around frantically, yelling at everyone, or to disappear, despondent, to corners of the house. Other times, she was in absolute rages. We never knew what caused them, but during those episodes, my dad would leave the house for days on end, and my sister and I would be left to deal with Mom, my younger brother joining in as he became old enough to try and help.

My sister would quietly approach her and say, "It's okay, Mom. Everything will be fine," and my mom would scoop her up and cradle her in her arms as she cried. My body recoiled when my mother's moods shifted from one extreme to another. With Dad gone, she would often try to engage me, and I typically responded with defiance to her rages and apathy to her depression and crying spells.

Not until I was about twelve did I learn of my mother's decades-long sexual abuse history at the hands of the husband of one of her older sisters. The molestation began when my mother was a young teenager and continued into her marriage to my father and the birth of us girls. It seemed as if Mom had had enough by the time I was entering puberty and had disclosed the abuse to her family—only to find it was something they were apparently aware of and wanted my mother to stay silent about. Having more of an understanding of what had happened for her increased my compassion for her, but the situation was a struggle, especially since we girls were still being carted around by my Aunt Maria-Theresa (who was exceptionally mean but mercifully not the wife of my mother's abuser) to visit family.

I had to force my body to hug and kiss every single grown-up I encountered, even the ones that smelled nauseatingly of alcohol and cigarettes. I had to smile and *represent* my parents at family functions even though I knew the truth of the relatives' betrayal and protection of the predator. It almost became unbearable for me to do so after I asked my father why my mother's relatives chose to not believe her. I asked my dad about it when he was out in the garage, and he didn't even look up from his work bench as he explained that they believed my mother but had chosen secrecy to protect the family's reputation. He said my grandmother had announced she would rather my mother die than shame the family by telling this secret. I walked away from the garage knowing there was something deeply wrong with the world and the people in it.

CHAPTER III

Crossing the Threshold

When I got the email from James that I could have the apartment for up to three months, I let out a huge sigh of relief. Paul and I had been navigating the house with difficulty, and I continued to sleep on an air mattress in the basement. As volatile as Paul and I could be with each other, I took solace in him being a loving father to the boys. He was a capable parent, and I was grateful not to have any safety concerns or worries about the boys being alone with him.

As I prepared to move out, the grieving process was overwhelming. On one cold and rainy day in March, as I lay on the couch in my office, I let the tears of loneliness and sorrow stream down my face, intermingling with the stained tears of all my clients. I cursed myself for doing this to my family, but my body would not let me entertain the idea of getting into bed with Paul and going back to our life. It was as though I was in a trance and could only move forward—but to where, I had no idea.

———

Paul and I quickly got into our new living arrangement and agreed to go back to our therapist even thought my heart wasn't in it. In sessions, I sat looking out the window as our therapist and Paul worked together to help him identify and label a feeling. I thought about what I wanted, who I wanted to be, and what life could be.

It felt selfish to ask myself these questions and yet absurd not to. When I wasn't with the kids, I was working full time and had a busy practice. My clients seemed to respond to my straight talk and dedication to them—the approach that had served me well with patients at the hospital. When I left the office, I would cry in parks and empty schoolyards before I headed back to the apartment. Some of the tears were about regret, and so many of them were about fear and shame. But slowly, every day, I could feel my body begin to uncurl itself a little bit more, and my breathing grew steadier. Even through the pain, I sipped tea and read good books, creating a quiet little oasis in the chaos of my life and a break from full-time parenting and the limbo of my separation.

Yoga

In the early morning hours, I would go to my gym only to rest my weary body in the sauna for a few moments. While lying there naked on a towel, my mind would wander to all the other hardships in my life: how tough growing up in my family had been, surviving my mother's wildness and my father's disappearing acts, navigating the childhood-spawned demons that plagued my sister and brother. I was beginning to believe I was doomed to a life of struggle and suffering.

My thinking was intense and never ended. I was showering three times a day just to focus on the water beating against my back instead of the torturing thoughts in my head. When I was sick of showering, I would drag myself outside to walk, focusing on my steps to distract myself from despair. Over the weeks, the cool and rainy March turned into a nicer April, and I would throw on a few layers, put in earbuds, and walk around the city listening to

Leonard Cohen's "Hallelujah" on repeat. These walks would last hours, and occasionally I would stop to use a public restroom to stretch out my hips and then keep walking. On these walks, with music as the backdrop, my mind flooded with memories of Paul and the kids, happy moments as well as dark ones. I felt I was watching two movies at the same time. And I started doing yoga. I was never interested in it before, found it too slow, and was put off by how trendy it was. But my body was sore, and my hips ached from the hours of aimless walking.

One day, while walking around Bloor Street and Dovercourt Road, I saw a sign for a free yoga trial at a nearby studio and decided to check it out. The place *felt* right. It was open, airy, and simple, with one hot room and one regular room and few bells and whistles. I came back the next day, not knowing what to expect. People trickled in, all ages, sizes, shapes, and outfits. It might seem silly to care about the aesthetics of the studio or makeup of the participants, but it was important for me. I was trusting my body as a thermostat, gauging my comfort level based on the authenticity I perceived. I was trusting it.

I settled on my back waiting for the class to start and in came Stevie, the instructor. Stevie did not look like what I thought a yoga teacher looked like. He was in his thirties and had what would be classified as a "dad bod," but he was strong as hell, holding poses with an enormous amount of power and flexibility. He was centered as he took charge of the class, leading us through poses. I was grateful he wasn't one of these ethereal, soft, waifish yoga instructors talking about the sun and the stars. I wanted to sweat, I wanted to feel strong, and I wanted to move. Stevie delivered, and his class was hard, really hard. The class was so challenging that it quieted every voice and worry in my head and forced me to focus on my body and my breathing. I loved it. It helped that Stevie was also a little bitchy, letting loose the occasional swear word or crass joke, but I could also feel his passion and dedication to yoga and the care he took in his practice and with his clients—my favorite combination.

After that first class, I signed up for a membership and spent more time moving and stretching my body on the mat and less time walking the city in despair. It felt so good. I tried out different classes and teachers, and realized what I liked and what I didn't care for. One Sunday evening, alone in the apartment and feeling a crushing weight from missing my kids, I jogged down to the studio to see if I could take a restorative yoga class I had heard about but didn't know anything about. The class was intimate. The lights were dim, candles lit in the middle of the room, and a gorgeous blonde woman with what looked like henna tattoos up and down her arms invited me to "take my space" in the room. I could feel my back stiffen, as if I was completely out of my place in this contrived setting. The instructor explained there would be five poses in the seventy-five-minute class. I broke into a sweat immediately. I did not want to rest in one pose for any longer than ten seconds. I did not want to be in my head or in my body, which is why I loved Stevie's class and his personality. His speed and manner allowed me to feel comfortable while my body and mind were doing the unfamiliar and historically uncomfortable: being still and flowing. But tonight, something deep inside me glued my ass to that mat, and I stared dumbly at this blonde angel. As the twelve of us lay on the mat in the soft darkness, a beautiful sound filled the air—the music of nature sounds, chimes, bells, and the wind. A deep peace came over me, and at the same time, a rush of tears. It felt like grief.

The instructor was seated in the corner of the room and directed us to lie on our mats with a block between our shoulder blades in a pose to open our hearts. Lying in this pose, my heart thrust upward and my body splayed, taking up space, brought more weeping. This time I couldn't make sense of my response. I felt I was an observer of my body, but my mind couldn't decipher the emotions. Then came another pose, a fetal type of position with a bolster between the knees. I instinctively pulled the prop blanket up and over my head, enveloping myself like in a womb and more tears flowed. I felt like Abe, who in the last few weeks before I moved out had insisted in being wrapped from head to toe in his muslin blankets. I intuitively knew he was sheltering himself from the outside world crumbling around him with our family's dissolution.

The more I thought about Abe and Jesse, the more I wept. I wasn't sure if those around me could hear—I was hoping they were in their own cocoons of healing and oblivious to mine. In this little bundle, I felt myself tiny and vulnerable. At the same time, in that moment, I felt all the fear, anger, uncertainty, and sadness that my body and mind had been through. I felt a sense of *coming home to myself* and a realization that I was no longer in the world trying to figure it all out. My body relaxed, knowing that I wasn't confined to the basement floor with Paul pacing above me anymore. I was small and safe in my bundle, and I could let go and rest.

A New Paradigm

The next few weeks at James's home went by with me weeping at yoga, crying nearly every day, and crying in bed every evening. One night, I felt so terribly alone, I scrounged in the back of James's closet and found one of his plaid shirts. I wrapped myself in it and climbed into the bed. I just needed something other than myself on my skin. As I struggled to breathe between terrified sobs, I smelled him on his shirt. He smelled like protection, and I felt his kindness envelope me while I bawled into the pillow. Paul and I communicated sporadically about the kids, and his messages to me veered from kind and apologetic to wildly angry and accusatory. I just cried. And I found myself being led toward a new kind of therapy.

My friend Melissa, who had left my previous therapist well before he had told me to get back in bed with Paul, had been seeing Adam's wife, Caren, for Eye Movement Desensitization and Reprocessing (EMDR) and somatic therapy, and said she was "done with therapy that requires talking to anyone about anything." She said her work with Caren had "changed my life and organized my mind," just from having fingers wave in front of her face and tap her kneecaps while images of her horrific childhood flashed before her eyes and through her body. I'd heard about EMDR, but in hospital training, that was sloughed off, and we continued with prescribing medication and teaching people to record and analyze their thoughts.

Melissa was a fellow social worker, and we shared the same education and professional background, so I was surprised she was seeing a therapist like Caren. "You have to try it," she had insisted a while back. "It's deprogramming me from the therapy we've been trained to do." I thought Melissa had finally come undone, that she was deranged and wasting her money. At the time, I politely wished her well, but once I had left my therapist, I was considering trying something different. One day, after a slew of angry texts from Paul, I felt desperate enough to ask Melissa for Caren's contact information. Caren, it turned out, was on maternity leave, but her husband, Adam, would be free to work with me. I booked my session with him for the following week.

The Work

After that profound initial session, Adam and I began working together once every two weeks. I was glad we didn't spend too much time on the narrative of my childhood and family history. I was exhausted from years of being trapped in that story with my previous therapist and going over my mother's swings from depressed to abusive and out-of-control behavior. I no longer wanted to explore the impact of my father's limited ability to protect me or be a leader in our family. Adam had told me that I didn't need to *talk* about my history, that he could see it in how it manifested in my body and my relational patterns.

Around Adam's office, beyond the beautiful couches and basin of water, there were also baskets of blankets and pillows, along with foam bats, sparing pads, and mats. When I asked about them, he explained they were tools and materials he used to re-create triggering experiences for his clients to move through, ways to release anger, frustration, sadness, or any old emotions they were storing in their bodies. I had read about some of these "cathartic" experiences in therapy where clients scream at a doll or punch a pillow and pretends it's their abuser. I thought it was gimmicky and told Adam so. He smiled and said, "Yeah, there's a lot of hokey practices out there. I'd stay away from that kind of work if the therapist is just triggering the trauma without dual awareness of the present moment of safety."

"What do you mean by dual awareness?" I asked.

"When the trauma occurred in your early life, you were a dependent child with few if any resources to assist you in surviving the experience," Adam explained. "What you did have, what we all have, is a nervous system wired for survival, designed to protect us. In an extreme emotional state, chaotic environment, or abusive situation, the emotional part of your brain will split from the logical, present moment part of the brain, allowing the child to tolerate or survive the event without shattering the psyche. It's what allows "the intolerable to be tolerable."

I nodded, understanding how Adam's explanation seemed to fit with many of my clients with sexual abuse histories.

Adam continued. "It's good that we can do this. However, the traumatic experience of the event becomes stored in the nervous system with a broken link to the present moment. This means the body doesn't know the event has ended, and it stays open on a loop and can be triggered in the future bringing up the same sensations, beliefs, and reactions."

"Okay," I said, not following all of it but realizing I could probably read about it free on the internet rather than pay him to teach it to me during our sessions.

Adam seemed to notice my skepticism and said gently, "I would invite you to be curious and open to what emerges in our work. The dual attention part is important because we need to create a bridge between the present-day part of the brain and the old trauma in the emotional brain so there can be an *update* and opportunity for a new, adaptive way of responding to the world. Being in the world."

I nodded. I'd try anything.

———

As Adam was teaching me about my nervous system, Paul and I had settled into the nesting plan with the kids. Throughout this time, Paul still vacillated between sending me texts and emails that wanted me home to work on our marriage and others that raged at me for destroying our family. I was grateful Jesse and Abe seemed to respond to the new routine well despite mistakenly calling me Daddy on the first transition day. On occasion, Jesse told me he was sad, and he wanted me and Daddy home at the same time. Abe seemed not to notice Paul and I weren't in the same room at the same time. On the days I wasn't occupied with being their mother, I was crying on my yoga mat or busying myself with an influx of clients and my practice.

The only bright time in my week was my emerging friendship with James. Our connection started slowly—an email from him that someone would be by to check the water heater, a question from me about a package that arrived for him. On the day he came by to pick up the mail, I invited him in for tea. James didn't talk much but he was an attentive listener and seemed to live fully in his body, calmly taking in my stories and seemingly in no hurry to be anywhere else. He made me feel calm in my own body, allowing me to slow my mind. In his company, for fleeting moments, I would forget that my life was a mess.

We had a few teas over the next month, and during our talks, I liked listening to myself laugh as I told him stories about who I was before marriage, before kids, before everything with Paul. I appreciated the sound of the girl I described to James. I loved her courage, her energy, and her humor. I also began to enjoy the way James looked at me. It made me feel pretty, which I hadn't felt in a long time. I was glad he was gay because it felt safer, acceptable to play at feeling pretty without any confusing influences while I was sorting out my marriage and next steps. But I knew I was on borrowed time. Paul was losing his patience with me, and I was no closer in deciding my future in our family.

The Wedding Incident

I got curious about myself, like Adam suggested. I reflected on my issues with trust and explored why I was so fiercely private and self-isolating. I had done enough therapy to know it was related to what I had come to call the Wedding Incident. But it was only through the new paradigm Adam was introducing me to that I understood the same urgency, and that the same feelings of mistrust and rage in my body were the same from that day. I let my mind float back.

––––––

Unbeknownst to me, Mom became a born-again Christian when I was fifteen years old. I had been raised Catholic, sort of, even though my father didn't go to church, having issues with all of the church's hypocrisy. My religion was outsourced to my mean Aunt Maria-Theresa, who dragged me and my sister to churches all over the city. At the age of seven, I remember complaining that my father never had to go to church, and my mother said it was because he'd had "a bad experience with the nuns back home." One day, when my dad was out in his garage, I brought him his hot coffee and sat on a stool, watching him smoke one cigarette after another and build his new project.

"Mom says you don't go to church because of the nuns. Is that true?" I asked. He smiled to himself and said, "Mean people, those church people." He sipped his coffee and added, "Always asking for money and terrifying everyone about their sins; meanwhile, they're the meanest of the bunch." He didn't say more about it, sent me on my way, and went back to hammering.

But I wished that, as a teenager, I could have been better prepared for when my mom shifted into saying things like, "I could never do this in the flesh. It's only by God's grace." My dad would murmur something back and escape to the garage with his cigarettes. Her new faith did seem to make her calmer, and she had stopped ranting at me in the car like she used to. Instead, she was using the car rides to teach me about Jesus, how he had forgiven those who crucified him, and how he was sitting at the right hand of the Father. I would look at her as if she had lost her mind. She would continue, saying, "The flesh holds anger and pain, but through Jesus I can forgive and move on. We all can." I stared out the window.

I had to admit things had been quieter at home with my mom walking around praying and reading her Bible—weird but quiet. So, I didn't think anything when my mother told me that my aunt would be taking my siblings and me to a family wedding, which surprised me considering we hadn't been to one in the years since my mother's family disowned her.

I hadn't seen Aunt Maria-Theresa in years and I hadn't missed her, but when she pulled up with her husband, my Uncle Nelson, in their Oldsmobile with my two cousins crammed in the back, I plastered a smile on my fifteen-year-old face as my fourteen-year-old sister and eight-year-old brother and I piled on top of them. The seven of us drove up to the big Portuguese wedding halls in Mississauga—a loud and hot car ride. When we got to the reception room, I was surprised to spot some cousins I hadn't been around in years. They seemed happy to see me, which made me think the evening might go well. There was no talk about my mother nor the fact that we hadn't seen each other for so long; instead, we did what kids and teenagers do: ran around chasing each other and gossiping.

After about an hour, it was time to find our seats and have dinner. I had missed the big Portuguese feasts at family gatherings, so I eagerly sat down and reached for the big breadbasket. That's when I felt like someone was staring at me from the next table. I looked up and saw *him*. "Him" was my mother's abuser, the man who had married my mother's other sister, Aunt Ana. He was sitting next to her and their two daughters with his eyes fixed on me. I couldn't place the expression on his face or the meaning behind the look, but I didn't care. I was too preoccupied with my rage at feeling betrayed by my mother. *Coward* was the word that came to mind about my parents.

My mind flashed to all the hours held hostage in family therapy when we were young, where my mother cried about the loss of her "family" even though my dad and we kids sat next to her. It was as if we were ghosts, and she didn't seem to include us in her definition of "family." The family therapist would spend the hour putting my mother back together while my little sister wept next to me, my father stared off into space, and I sat seething, furious that the grown-ups in my life were useless and oblivious when it came to managing themselves. *What a waste of goddamn time* was the thought that kept going through my young head—then and at the reception. What a waste of tears, anger, therapy, sadness, rage, thought, grief, and betrayal. All those years lost in pain for my mother to turn around and seat me four feet away from a pedophile.

I got a hold of myself and finished buttering my bread as I looked around my table to see if I had an ally, an adult who could explain what was happening. There were none. I decided to carry on eating and go about the rest of the wedding keeping to myself—until I realized my little brother was no longer sitting at the table. I started worrying. That worry turned to panic when I looked up and saw that "my uncle" was also gone. I interrupted the grown-ups and in my broken Portuguese asked where my brother had gone. I was ignored. I ran from table to table looking for him as thoughts of my brother being molested flashed through my head. My hands were sweaty, my heart pounded, and my mind raced. He wasn't anywhere in the dining room, so I burst into the hallway, running toward the bathrooms, where I found him splashing happily in the sink with another little boy I didn't know. I grabbed him by the arm hard, yanking him out into the hall. He looked terrified. I was able to break out of my anger and gave him a hug, telling him to always let me know where he was going. I then went outside to have my first cigarette, as I had seen my father do when he needed a break from everyone. It was easy enough to bum one from the teenagers smoking. I let them light it and walked over to the side of the building alone, inhaling and exhaling as if I had been doing it all my life.

When I got back to the table, I also decided to have my first drink. No one seemed to notice that a fifteen-year-old was drinking. They were too busy mingling, dancing, and judging each other. I started picking up all the half empty glasses of wine on my table, then the table next to me, and the table next to that. I felt like that was what you did when you'd been betrayed. I got hammered. That would have been fine if I had stayed in my seat and gone to sleep, but I didn't. Instead, I hit the dance floor alone, swinging my arms wildly and moving my body in strange ways. People moved away from me, but I didn't care. I then stumbled over to some cousins of mine, said hi, and they backed away. I was unbothered. I started wobbling around the hall aimlessly until I saw "my uncle" looking at me through the corner of his eye while he talked to a group of people.

I walked directly up to him and Aunt Ana and the group of people they were standing with. I didn't say a word. I stood there, staring. I was too inebriated to fully take in what was happening, but I could sense everyone's discomfort except for his. He seemed to have no problem ignoring me completely. Aunt Ana finally turned, and he followed her. I followed them both. The two of them and I, by their side, walked to another table, to the dance floor, to the bar, and finally to the coat check where they had had enough and were ready to leave. The room was beginning to spin, and I was only faintly aware people were following me and whispering, probably trying to figure out what to do but finding this too bizarre to have a clear action plan. I didn't care because I focused on him. Aunt Ana started crying and soon a small crowd huddled around her and moved her away. Then it was me and him at the coat check. All at once everything seemed to slow down. Then, he turned around to look at me and calmly asked, "Do I know you?"

I felt as if I had been punched in the stomach. I felt very blurry, with a drunken sensation in my body, and my lungs were tight and sore from that stupid cigarette. My head was spinning, and the loudness of the hall music hurt my brain. All of a sudden, I was embarrassed by all the people staring at me and ashamed that my aunt was screaming and crying as she was being ushered out of the room. He was unfazed and walked right by me, collecting his hysterical wife on the way out the door. Then I threw up. I kept throwing up all the way to my Aunt Maria-Theresa's Oldsmobile and was only semiconscious of the insults she was shrieking at me in Portuguese. My Uncle Nelson was muttering prayers under his breath while my two cousins were smirking. My sister and brother looked worried for me. I slumped onto the floor of the backseat.

I couldn't stop vomiting. My mother was holding my hair as I wretched into the toilet. I didn't notice that she was crying for a few minutes as I was more focused on whether or not I was dying. She started praying out loud. "Forgive me, God, forgive me," she said over and over again while she looked up at the ceiling and made the sign of the cross. She then turned her attention back to me and cried, "I feel so horrible that you did this to protect me."

In that moment, every ounce of respect I might have ever had for my mother was expelled out of me into the toilet. I was done. I knew in that moment that she would never be the woman and mother I needed her to be, that she needed herself to be. I was on my own and that was fine, preferable in fact. I wiped my mouth and using all the energy I had left in my fifteen-year-old body, propped myself up and looked her in the eye. "I didn't do it for you—I did it for me," I told her, and continued puking until I blacked out.

God in My Pocket

Over the next few weeks, things were relatively quiet between Paul and me. I started taking even better care of myself, spending more time outdoors on long walks around the city listening to beautiful music, taking daily yoga classes, and making myself and the children healthy meals with fresh produce from spring farmers' markets. I also started thinking more about a future outside of my marriage. On my walks, I started seeing For Sale signs on residences, and the spring real estate market was well underway. I popped my head into a few open houses but got scared off by the high listing prices for small homes that needed a lot of work. I wanted to live in the city because I didn't drive—having been born and raised downtown, I never needed to—but having walked away from the hospital and its steady income, benefits, and pension, I didn't even know if I could afford to stay.

At night, I would lose sleep over financial anxiety. I woke up feeling nauseous and frightened of being alone. I worried about the state of my worrying. I knew not to stay in bed, that it was best for my mental health to get outside and walk. I was losing more weight with all this walking, and my clothes were hanging from my newly lean frame. I walked long distances, feeling worse instead of better as all I seemed to see were young families strolling the streets and enjoying the fresh air. Thoughts of Paul and the boys flooded me. I was choosing to be alone, which was the reason for my current misery. My choices were hurting the boys. It seemed that instead of this separation, we should be like these strangers my eyes followed who were out getting ice cream and going to the park. For hours, I fought with myself, moving quickly through neighborhoods, hoping to keep ahead of the overpowering feelings of guilt and shame.

It was getting cold and dark. As I was looking to jaywalk Bloor Street en route to my place, a little commotion caught my eye. A woman about my age pulled back from two young men, irritated, shooting them dirty looks as she hurried away. The men seemed surprised and hurt by her reaction to them. One looked to be in his early twenties, tall, wearing a black baseball hat with a gold plate on the front with JESUS in bold lettering. The other was shorter, darker skinned, and stocky. The two of them studied the crowd. They tried to hand a green envelope to a woman passing by. She, too, looked annoyed and withdrew. I found myself amused by how confused the young men looked, and I felt bad about the reactions they were getting.

Since my mother was a born-again Christian and I attributed the betrayal at the wedding to her relationship with her savior, I wasn't open to the church or God. I only trusted what I could see, touch, smell, hear, and taste with the physical senses. But I was lonely after spending the day at war with myself, so I walked over. "Hi," I said, tapping the taller one on the back. "Can I help you guys with anything?"

He turned to look at me and immediately jumped back as if he'd seen a ghost.

"Is that a green jacket you're wearing?" the shorter guy asked me.

"You could call it olive." I glanced down.

They exchanged huge grins.

"Did you see us trying to talk to that woman in the green trench coat just now?" the taller one asked.

"Yeah, I guess so," I said, beginning to wish I had minded my own business.

"Well, this might sound strange to you, but I have the gift of prophesy," said the short guy. "When I woke up this morning, God told me that I was to write this down and hand it to a woman wearing green today."

He handed me the envelope, which I opened to find a green postcard. "Does this make sense to you?" he asked. It read:

*Today you got up and wanted to hear something dif-
ferent. This is it. You are loved, beautiful, and worth
all the attention. I see financial provision coming your
way, whether you have plenty or are in need. You are
coming into a place of contentment. You have all you
need because you have love and are loved.*

I cried and couldn't stop. I felt an opening in my chest and a warmth
moving through me, a tingling up and down my spine. I knew this
was real, I knew it was for me, but at the same time my head couldn't
wrap itself around the experience.

"Want a side hug?" the Jesus-hat-wearing guy asked me sincerely.

"No, no, I'm all right," I said. "Thank you very much for this." The
men offered small bows and walked off down the street with smiles
on their faces. Crossing the street, disoriented, I almost got hit by a
car. My eyes were full of tears and I carried a letter from God deep
in my pocket.

———

I started paying attention to some of the reading Adam assigned
me that seemed to speak to this connection between humans and
a *Source*, or what I was calling God. I also slowly shared the news
about the separation to a mix of responses. One mom-friend at the
kids' school sucked in her breath, squeezed my arm, and whispered,
"You are so brave." Others couldn't seem to get away quickly enough,
as if separation was contagious. Strangely, some responded that
I should party and "Get out there and have some fun!" What others
thought seemed to matter less to me than it had in the past. My
body continued to tell me what felt right, which was to sit alone
in James's beautiful house and read, go for walks, and head to the

yoga studio to cry and breathe. I saw James every once in a while, enjoying his company and finding myself wanting more time with him. I was careful to stay mindful that I had enough relationship problems on my hands and not to become dependent on anyone.

Decided

Paul and I were separated, but that didn't mean we had made the decision to divorce. I didn't know what to do, so I did nothing; I didn't know what to say, so I said nothing. When I couldn't do that, I took a shower—I knew it was hard to make any life-altering choices from the shower. But one day, I received a text message from Paul: The marriage was over.

He was tired of waiting for me to decide. He was tired of waiting for me to participate in therapy. He was tired. So was I. It had been almost six months since my body refused to be wife and mother in the same way. I was exhausted by being at my new growing practice every day, by the endless walks around the city and the hours of crying on my yoga mat, by the mental weight of not knowing what was going to happen among Paul, my family, and me. Too many voices were in my head, and I still couldn't get clear on my next step. I looked up in the mirror, and saw a young woman looking back at me, relieved. I exhaled.

––––––––

Within two weeks of Paul's text ending our marriage, I firmed up plans by securing a lawyer and buying a house. I was working with a realtor but had an impulse one day to get online myself and spotted one that seemed to call out to me. It was a sweet, little two-bedroom townhouse on the same street as the boys' school. My realtor told me it was a miracle this place was available and priced to sell. The house did need some cleaning up and renovating to be a fit for the boys and me, but I wasn't worried about the work. My entire childhood was spent with one or another room in our house cordoned off by plastic as my dad worked away to transform it into a masterpiece with custom cabinetry and mosaic ceilings. I felt as if I had been underwater these last months, and I wanted to move fast. Figuring that Paul would stay in our family home and buy me out, I made an offer and it was accepted. I then began to ask around for a contractor.

Meanwhile, Paul and I barely spoke. Through a colleague, I found a lawyer, Susan, who was quick, smart, and didn't pull any punches. She moved Paul's attorney along in completing the separation agreement, explaining to me that I would need to have the finances sorted through to apply for a mortgage that would pay for the house I bought without any conditions. She told me that although it was *gutsy* to buy the house, it was equally stupid, and I should consult her on these decisions. Emboldened by the decision to divorce, I felt I could navigate any issue and figure it out. I put all my focus on separating from Paul and working out a parenting schedule. When I wasn't busy setting up my new life, I was tending to my current one with the kids and work. I had stopped talking to any friends, seeing that people weren't supportive when they asked about my situation. Instead, they were looking for clues about the state of their own marriage and felt far too comfortable giving their opinion when it wasn't requested. I went to yoga almost every day, and on the mat my body would let down, my thoughts would quiet, and the tears would flow. Even though I was invigorated by the forward momentum of my life, I had much to grieve, and yoga was the only place I seemed able to do that.

CHAPTER IV

Allies and Enemies

"Paul signed the papers," read my lawyer's email. A huge relief came over me, as I had been expecting an all-out war with Paul, who wasn't speaking to me. Within a month, our separation agreement was done, our finances sorted through, and my mortgage approved as Paul bought our family home from me, enabling me to secure a down payment for the townhouse. I was surprised by the speed of the process, but it seemed that Paul wanted to move on as quickly as I had.

My time at James's house was coming to an end. I had been living there for three months and found myself thinking about him when I needed respite from my busy, stressful days. In focusing on him, I was appreciating the version of myself I was when he was around. I liked that me. I wasn't trying to impress or entertain him. I was enjoying myself and saw him take pleasure in my company. Those few times we had tea at the house felt wonderful. I realized that what I liked so much about James, besides looking at him, was that he asked nothing of me and valued who I was. My mind drifted back to a time when Paul and I were like that, but I brought my attention back to the images and thoughts of James and the kindness in his eyes when he looked at me. I knew he would extend the rental of his house if I asked, but it had been three months living there, and the time had come for me to move out of this cocoon and build a life for myself and the boys.

Child Support

I closed on my townhouse at the end of August, but it needed renovating and an updated bathroom that could work for me and the boys. I had thought to ask Paul to continue with our nesting arrangement and staying at the house until the renovations were completed, but he was grumbling about finances. All of our monies had been separated, and we had worked out child support. I felt grateful and guilty about receiving child support. My lawyer waved away my guilt. "He makes three times what you make, and in his career, he is on course to make four times what you make," she said. "And didn't you support him through several different career paths, his studying, and the start of his business when he had no income?"

"Yes," I said, "but I'm moving on and want nothing from him."

"Don't be dumb," she responded. "Don't make life harder for yourself than it has to be," and she closed the matter.

My brother agreed when I shared with him the guilt I was feeling. He told me he understood, but that I should keep in mind that our grandmothers and the generations of women before were forced to stay in marriages because they had no other options. "Honor them," he urged, "and make a future for yourself and the boys with that money."

Ally

"You need to meet Trevor," said Sarah, one of the moms at the school, when I told her about my new house. "And I think you should date him. You two would be perfect for each other."

"Yeah, thanks, but I just need a contractor," I said.

"Okay, okay, but still speak to Trevor. He's the only person I trust with my house," she said as she gave me his number. "He's super busy and prefers to work in the East End of the city, but I'm sure he'll do it for you."

"Why?"

"Because I've already told him about you," she said with a wink.

"What! What did you say to him about me?"

"Calm down, calm down. I've known him for years and he's always dating disaster women trying to be some kind of hero. I keep telling him he needs to be with an independent woman who's smart and has her shit together, and I mentioned you when I heard about your separation."

I rolled my eyes at her complete ignorance that she was attempting to set up Trevor with another woman who did not have her shit together. But the new house needed help, so I shut my mouth and messaged Trevor.

———

As I approached my new house, I saw a tall man staring up at the front window. "Trevor?" I asked.

The man who turned to face me was handsome. Not James or model handsome, but grown-up man handsome. "Natasha, good to meet you. What do you want to get done?" he asked, jumping right to the work.

He had a calmness that felt like he had earned it, as though he had seen everything and would no longer let the world disturb his peace.

I was talking to him about needing new bathrooms when I heard myself say, "You see, I need this done quickly because my marriage is over, and I feel I've been in the dark, so now I need lots of light, so I want pot lights, pot lights, pot lights everywhere." I realized I was swinging my hands in the air.

"Okay, well, we'll see," he said. "I don't usually come around to the West End, but our mutual friend said you were in a jam." I took a breath and got a hold of myself, softening.

"Yeah, I'm moving in soon. My father can do renovations, but our relationship is complicated, and my ex-husband wants me out so I'm kind of on my own here."

I led Trevor from room to room, gesturing to all the things I wanted painted, removed, added on, or redone. He followed me looking at where I pointed and would say, "Okey dokey." As we were winding down the tour, I looked more closely at him. Trevor was maybe midforties and had a deep, tanned complexion; dark, short hair; and big, broad shoulders. He was over six feet tall and was a powerful-looking man with kind, gentle eyes and a slow and steady way about him. I liked that he didn't flinch when I swore or was provocative or inappropriate. In fact, he seemed rather amused when I let a "motherfucker" or "bullshit" fly. He just shook his head and chuckled. He wasn't making fun of me or judging me; instead, he was enjoying me.

"So, will you do it?" I asked.

"Not to worry," Trevor said, with no reaction to my oversharing. "We'll take care of you." My heart stopped with the words *we'll take care of you*. I knew it was an expression and that he probably said it to all his customers, but hearing it made something tug inside me.

Experiencing Me

I was packing up to leave James's place. My three months were up, and I was moving to another apartment to await the readiness of my new house. I had found a sweet little main floor of a house, a few blocks from the kids' school off Harbord Street, where we would be for the six weeks it would take to renovate. As I packed and lifted heavy boxes, I could feel each of my muscles. I had been getting to know my body for what felt like the first time in my life. I loved the strength and flexibility that yoga and rest had given me these last few months. I was no longer crying on my mat during yoga class, reveling instead in the heat of the room and the challenge of each pose. I was impressed by my strength. I felt light, healthy in my little body.

———

Moving day was the coming weekend, and James stopped by to visit me at his place. We had been spending time together more regularly and had settled into a comfortable friendship. He would sit at the table eating the dinner I had prepared, listening, while I told him the goings-on of my day and funny stories from my past. I was learning more about him and the way he experienced life. He was a beautifully sensitive person who had kept to himself and was mostly isolated from the harshness of the world and being with other humans. I was grateful to him for the little cocoon his home had provided for me and the re-experiencing of myself through his eyes.

I also learned that he wasn't gay. In fact, he threw his gorgeous head back and let out a huge belly laugh when I told him that was what I had been thinking all these tea times. He said it was too bad that a handsome and meticulous man who was respectful of women and emotionally attuned was automatically assumed as gay. I agreed, but

I was also glad my mistake had allowed me to focus more on feeling pretty and alive for myself instead of trying to attract or impress him. I thanked him with my whole heart for his kindness. He gave me a big hug, told me it was his pleasure and that he was thinking of a career as a therapist, wanting to be with people in a way that was authentic and real, and wanted to support others in healing. "We need more therapists like you that let us experience ourselves in the world with such safety and connection," I told him as I said goodbye.

I moved into my last apartment with no trouble, as I had nothing to haul but some clothes for me and the boys and a few of their toys and books. The day Paul officially closed on our matrimonial house was also the day he changed the locks, which I thought was dramatic and unnecessary. We had had little to no contact in the last two months other than when he called my phone to Facetime with the kids every evening. We wouldn't speak. I would hand Jesse the phone. The truth was, I would have preferred that he didn't call to speak to the kids every night because it seemed intrusive and disruptive. I even noticed that the boys often didn't want to take the phone and although I didn't like how uncomfortable it made me to see Paul on the screen, I kept my mouth shut. This was a transition time, and it was good for both of us to stay connected to the kids. I would continue to shift my focus from my past with Paul to creating my own life and future.

Don't Worry, We Fix

"Okey dokey," Trevor said each time I made a change in the plans for the renovations. The phrase sounded so funny coming out of this big, gruff man, and it slayed me. Trevor and I had been hanging out almost every day when I'd come check on the house. He'd always come outside with me, light a cigar, and suggest we go get coffee for his crew.

On a scorching hot afternoon at the end of August, I was watching him puff on his cigar. "So, tell me more about yourself," Trevor said with a grin, a circle of aromatic smoke encircling him.

"What do you want to know?" I said, balancing the coffees we were bringing back for his men.

"Well, I don't know. Anything, everything. I like you talking to me," he said. "Most people can't keep my attention."

"You're lucky," I replied. "Most people make sure they get my attention."

He chuckled and sipped his coffee. As I drank mine, I thought about the differences among Paul, James, and Trevor. I wondered what it was that had me choose Paul as my husband and not someone gentle and emotional like James or steady and reliable like Trevor. Why was it that twenty-four-year-old me was attracted to the chaos of my relationship with Paul, our neediness and control of each other? I brushed the hair out of my eyes and came back to the present moment. Trevor had leaned up against a mailbox, watching me, a smile on his face.

"Can I help you with something?" I asked, not enjoying being stared at.

Trevor smiled. "You got some problems, girl," he said with a wink. "Don't worry, we fix."

———

It was a quiet, humid night outside, and my new apartment felt quiet and humid inside. I went to the refrigerator to pour myself a glass of wine and looked at the picture of the kids I had put on the door. I missed their little faces even though I had been with them just a few hours before and knew they were happy and safe with Paul. A little twinge of guilt crept up when I thought about the three of them. *Are you happy now? Happy to wreck your family and be irresponsible?* a voice in my head hissed. This voice came for me often, and I didn't like it. I much preferred the one I woke up to. In the mornings, I would approach the mirror with my cup of coffee and look at myself, watch the smile on my face, and admire my new, healthy yoga body. I had never been in such good shape, and I liked myself and the life I was creating.

Every day, I stopped by the new house, and Trevor was there organizing his guys and juggling his cell phone and cigar. It didn't matter how busy he was or whom he was talking to. Every time I walked in, he would excuse himself and turn his attention to me. "Hello," he'd say in his calm and confident way. "Nice to see you."

It made me laugh: the consistency of his greeting and the little routine developing between us.

"How are things looking?" I asked one day, looking up at his tall frame, blocking my eyes from the sun.

"Oh, you know, just perfect, just lovely. Everything is perfect."

I giggled. "I feel you would say that to me in that exact way even if we were standing here watching the house burn down."

"Probably," he said, "but it would be perfect, just fine. We'd just fix that one up for you and then we'd have more time to chat together."

I nodded. I enjoyed being with him to chat. But I felt my protectiveness over my new life. I stopped visiting the house as much for fear that Trevor—or anyone—would take away my independence.

Tug-of-War

Paul had been so quiet after the text message he sent ending our marriage that I believed the worst of our relationship was over, especially since the separation agreement and parenting schedule had been finalized and I was out of the marital home. So, I was surprised when I received a text from him calling me selfish for having the boys live in a rental, "displacing them" while I was renovating the new house. He said he had spoken to his lawyer about sending someone to come and inspect the living conditions to ensure it was suitable for the children.

"Don't bother responding" was my brother's advice.

"I don't understand what's going on with him," I said. "We're separated, done. Why doesn't he just leave me alone now?"

———

I sat on Adam's big, soft couch, waiting to hear what we were going to explore today.

The last few sessions had been about me sitting with and noticing sensations in my body, mostly heat, tightness, and pulsing energy. I hated doing this and found staying in my skin a challenge. After a few minutes, I would talk, asking questions about the neuroscience of somatic processing. Adam and I knew this was my way of avoiding the work, avoiding the pain that I knew was deep below. He gently brought that up during one session, adding that my questions were welcome and it was important for me to build trust with him and the process as I allowed myself to be increasingly vulnerable.

We had been working on issues of co-parenting with Paul, noticing the emotions in my body when his face showed up on the screen every night or when I received a text message from him calling me selfish and overriding our parenting plan. When I thought about that, my fists clenched, and my jaw tightened.

"Stand up," Adam said to me. "Today, you feel your anger," and he directed me to the pads, handing me a foam bat. I stood up, took a few swings, and felt how strong I was. Adam pressed me harder. "Swing and hit." I kept swinging, kept hitting, feeling the power in my body, the depth of the anger I held within me. Adam kept pushing, bringing up stories of my anger at Paul, the betrayals and mistreatment I had experienced in my life from my family and others. With each new narrative, I would feel an initial surge of anger, but soon the anger shifted and shame crept up, the belief I must be bad, given how the people who were supposed to love me felt about me. It had to be true that I was difficult, selfish, and angry. Look at how many people in my life had a problem with me. I felt I was going to be sick, felt a weakness in my knees as I kept swinging the bat, trying to keep up with the anger but slowing down with the shame. I began to feel hot and panicked, and I didn't want to hit anymore. I dropped the bat and crumpled to the floor, burying my head in my knees and covering my face with my hands as I sobbed. Adam was gently coaching me to breathe, to let the emotions come, all of them. I felt everything: rage, grief, shame, and intense sadness.

As my breathing steadied, I whispered, "I don't want to fight anymore." I felt so fragile. "Leave me alone, everybody leave me alone, I'm so tired," I whispered to everyone and no one.

"Yes, you're exhausted," Adam said gently. As he moved closer to me on the floor, I curled up tighter. He stopped, staying near but not advancing. I didn't want Adam to see me, to really see me. Adam began to hum, then softly sing in a beautiful language that sounded like Spanish, but I couldn't be sure. Regardless, it was comforting, soothing. I hugged my knees and began to sway. I was aware that, even though I didn't want to be seen, I also didn't want to be alone.

I thought about the movie *Traffic*, with Michael Douglas, which I once watched at a get-together. There's a scene where he goes looking for his daughter, who is strung out on drugs. He ends up finding her high, naked, and in bed with a man. The guy in the bed looks terrified and runs out of the room, and Michael Douglas rushes over to his nearly unconscious daughter, scooping her up, and holding her. My body recoiled in disgust watching that. "Eww, what's he doing? She's disgusting," I said aloud. One of my friends leaned over and whispered, "Dude, that's his daughter." I couldn't believe my reaction was that the girl was repulsive, that she deserved to lie in her own trauma because she was *bad*, and that only when she was ready to behave in a dignified manner should her parents love her again. There I was, curled up on Adam's floor in pain and fear, and wanting him not to look at me for the same reasons.

Over the next few sessions, Adam expertly moved closer to me on the floor, and then one day offered me a hug. I instinctively clasped my knees to my chest and told him, "No, don't touch me," as I had instructed friends in the past. Adam stepped back a little, giving me space and respecting my boundary but not leaving. As these sessions progressed and I came to trust he would respect my no, that I could say what I wanted and needed, I began to feel that I didn't want him to go away. Knowing I could choose it or not, I began to want comfort.

Attachments

I was finally moving into my new house, and Trevor had offered to help me move, but I declined, not wanting to lead him on. On his last day working on the house, he said, "Listen, I haven't wanted to spend time with someone in a long time, and I like being with you. I'm attracted to you and think we'd have a good time together."

It was honest and direct, no games, no baggage, and I was fond of Trevor. I felt secure and comfortable when I was around him. "I'm flattered, really," I said, "but I'm not ready."

"Well, a guy's got to ask, I suppose. Take care of yourself, and let me know if you change your mind."

"Thanks, Trevor," I said, knowing I was going to miss him and feeling a little emotional. "Really, thank you for everything."

"My pleasure," he said, giving me a wink and driving away.

I asked my dad if he could help me move my few boxes. My dad showed up in his truck and I clambered in, slamming the door behind me. "I only hear from you when you need something" was the first thing he said, blowing smoke out the crack of the car window.

I strained my head out the passenger window to get some fresh air, gearing myself up for the day ahead with him. My father's personality and mood shifted as much as my mother's did. Most of the time, he was lost in his own world of renovating and smoking, vacantly joining the family when Mom forced him to. I tended to interact with my father by bringing out coffee and pastries to him in the garage, my mother's way of employing us children to coax him into the family. She was always putting a bunch of grapes, slices of cheese, hot coffee, or a baked good into our hands and pushing us out the door to smile at our dad and tell him we loved him. I would step over the wintery ice in a thin shirt, useless against the cold, as I brought him his lunch and set it down on his worktable while he finished sawing.

This is the image forever ingrained in me about my father: cigarette firmly clamped in his mouth underneath his tobacco-stained mustache, smoke circling into his eyes while his hands were busy with a piece of wood or mixing plaster. Dad was a handsome man and very un-Portuguese looking, even though he'd been born on the Portuguese islands like my mother. My mom used to joke that people thought he was an alcoholic because his face had an inexplicable pink hue, but my father never touched a drop of alcohol after being raised by a violent alcoholic father. I would always point that out to my mother when she would murmur her disappointments about my dad. She would glare at me and rattle off more examples. At this point I would nod, not wanting to get her going. My father knew how to do this also: nod and get out of her way so he could slip back out to the garage.

As I got older, I refused my mother's demands for me to "connect" with my father, a boundary that would enrage her, sometimes causing her to blame me for my father's disinterest and isolation. I remember coming home from school one day and seeing my brother and sister, heads bowed, sitting at the kitchen island with tears running down their faces, as my mother waved wildly around the room, frantic and out of control. I looked at my father as he sat perched on his stool under the stove hood fan, the only place inside he was allowed to smoke—a concession of my mother, "or else we'd never see him." As my mom ranted and my younger siblings, ages seven and twelve, sat weeping in front of him, I remember thinking of my dad as a coward for letting this happen. That day, as I stood in the doorway, I was only thirteen years old, but I knew this was complete and utter madness. I turned to leave and my mother caught sight of me, ran to me, grabbed my arms, and pulled me over to my father, telling me my father was leaving and demanding that I tell him that I loved him, that I needed him to stay. I pulled my arms out of her grip and moved out of reach. She ignored me and ran to my brother and sister, yelling for them to declare their need for my father. "We love you, Daddy, please stay," came their quiet little voices from beneath their bowed heads. My mother screamed, "We love you. Stay. We need you to stay." I had had enough.

I left them there in the kitchen, walked away up to my bedroom, and picked up the phone, calling my friend D.J., who was a good listener. I asked if I could come to his house for dinner. All of a sudden, the receiver was yanked out of my hand. It landed on the floor with a crash as my mother threw me against the wall. She pinned me and snarled in my face with manic, dark eyes, screaming, "He's leaving because of you, because you only care about yourself." She yelled at me for a few more minutes, unintelligibly, and once she had exhausted herself, she let me go and left the room. I caught my breath and retrieved the phone from the floor—D.J. was still on the other end, his mother also on the line. "What's happening, dear?" she asked me. "Are you okay?

"Yeah, I'm fine," I muttered. "My mom's having a bad day." And I hung up.

Over the years I learned how to connect with my dad in a way that he could respond to. I would be quiet when he was quiet and talk when he wanted to talk. Now, as we moved into the new house, we navigated around each other silently, efficiently doing all the things that needed doing, and every once in a while exchanging words on politics or the other goings-on in the world. I was careful around my father in a way I wasn't around my mother. When we were done, he drove off with a small wave. I waved back and silently, in my heart, told him I loved him—the only safe way to express a feeling to my dad so as not to scare him off. Then I turned toward my new house.

———

I had been seeing Adam once every two weeks for four months, and I still found myself falling into periods of extreme emotion: either exhilaration and joy or sadness and anger. I was grateful I didn't have the boys all the time, meaning I could fall apart when they weren't with me instead of in front of them, as my mother had with us. I felt terribly alone during these low times. Adam had been teaching me to meditate, and I took my worries to my meditation pillow as well as my yoga mat. My meditation pillow was my bedtime pillow, propped up against the frame of my bed, where I'd sit on the floor cross-legged and lean back against the mattress, close my eyes, and attempt to still my mind. I hated it, but I was good at accomplishing tasks, so I willed myself to sit for ten minutes. By the time my timer went off, I realized I had spent the whole time replaying my problems in my head and planning out my grocery list. I didn't think I was doing it right.

"I don't know how to meditate," I complained to Adam during one of our sessions.

"Meditation isn't about clearing or quieting the mind. It's about stilling the Self to observe the mind," he said. He explained that the mind was meant to be a "problem solver," not a leader in our lives, and our overthinking had taken away from our ability to experience life. He explained that the body was for experiencing but was cut off from its partnership with the mind, keeping human beings from fully being in the world. With my continued practice of meditation, I became better at quieting the worries in my head.

The Ordeal

That same week of meditation teaching with Adam, as I was wrapping up my day at work and saying goodbye to my last client, I turned on my phone to see I had a voice message from the school, three missed calls from Paul, and several text messages, all sent within the last thirty-seven minutes. I called the school and the secretary let me know that Jesse had a stomachache and she thought he would be more comfortable at home. She also said that when she couldn't get a hold of me, she called Paul, and he had been right over and taken Jesse and Abe home. I thanked her and headed over to Paul's to pick up the kids.

Paul wouldn't let me see the boys. He believed I was picking myself, my life, my work over the children. As I fought with him at the threshold, I felt we were married again. He closed the door and left me outside alone, and he went back in with the kids. I felt crushing pain in my body, like the door closing had been a punch in the stomach, and flashed on a memory of another time a door had been closed on me by a man who left me alone outside while he went in to be with the family.

———

"Get dressed, wear something pretty," my mom called out to my sister and me. I was nineteen, and my mom was the only one excited about Christmas and going to church. She was taking the whole family, my little brother and father included, which was rare as they were usually exempt from these trips. My dad was in his usual place sitting by the oven fan smoking, and I asked him, "What's with Mom?"

"Who knows," came his sleepy reply, and he went back to smoking and muttering to himself. We piled into the car for church and headed to the Portuguese Roman Catholic church I had grown up in, playing angels in the procession and suffering through catechism classes. As the five of us walked into the church, I realized it wasn't a service; instead, we were at the church hall, which was crowded with Portuguese people yelling, waving, hugging, kissing, and drinking. My mother had over fifty first cousins, and I realized quickly that they and their families were the ones celebrating. I had not seen any of these people for over five years, not since the Wedding Incident, and I was stunned to see them there. "Mom, what are we doing here?" I asked.

She looked at me annoyed and said, "Don't be difficult; this is our family." My sister and brother bounded into the room, running off to play with cousins, unbothered by this change of events. My father shrugged his shoulders and ambled back outside to light a cigarette. I stood in the entranceway looking at all the people who had abandoned my mother and our family for telling the truth about her abuse. I stood there alone; no one spoke to me. Eventually, I wandered around the room and smiled at people I didn't recognize and steered clear of the people I did. Those who didn't know me smiled back; those who did stayed away. I knew why: Either they had been

Talk Therapy Isn't Enough

at the wedding and witnessed my behavior with the pedophile uncle or they'd heard about it. My parents and I never talked about that day, and I never heard my mom mention getting together with this side of the family again. I tried to look busy, but couldn't seem to land anywhere, so I spent most of the next hour taking myself in and out of the bathroom and different corners of the hall, pretending I was looking for something. I was seething at my mother for bringing us there without warning me. I was also confused as to what could possibly have changed our family's position on being among them.

Finally, it was time to eat, and I lined up silently next to relatives to fill my plate at the buffet line. *Now where to sit?* I thought to myself. As I carried my plate through the sea of long tables, I realized that there were no empty chairs. I had done a pretty good job of keeping myself calm and entertained these last few hours, but I just wanted to sit down. Some movement caught my eye at the back of the room, and I saw my little brother banging into people and my sister behind him, clumsily trying to maneuver themselves into some chairs. I made my way to my siblings and was relieved to see three empty chairs near them. Wordlessly, I sat down and began to eat. As I forked the first mouthfuls, I began to feel better and thought maybe I was being dramatic. This wasn't so bad.

Someone reached over for the empty chair next to me, and I looked up, hopeful I could talk to someone. A mixture of adrenaline from fear and rage surged through me. I was staring right up at *him*. I couldn't believe it. My mother had done this to me again. My uncle looked down, startled, not expecting to see me sitting there. He stood frozen for a second, until the man standing next to him, whom I didn't recognize, muttered in Portuguese "senta, senta," meaning to *sit down already*. Calmly and coolly, ignoring me completely, he sat and began eating, carrying on a conversation with the people next to him. I took two slow, long, deep breaths, pushed my chair out, and walked over to my father, who was sitting with a group of men. My dad glanced over his shoulder at me, and as I approached, he offered a casual "Hey."

"Dad, I don't have a seat," I said, my voice low and shaky.

He waved me away, pointing at other tables, saying, "What are you talking about? Go sit down."

"Dad, I don't have a seat," I said again, this time with power in my voice. This time he looked at me, then scanned the room for an empty chair.

"What do you mean you don't have a seat? Go and sit . . . " His voice trailed off as he saw where I had been sitting. My heart leaped into my chest, and I hoped my father would march us all out of there, outraged at my mother's betrayal. Instead, he said, "Oh, okay. Let's find you somewhere else to sit."

I glared at him and asked, "What are we doing here?" He stared down at his hands. I turned on my heel and walked out of the church, into the night air, in my thin party dress.

I was pacing in front of the church, a light snow falling on my bare head and arms. Even though it was freezing, I preferred being outside than in there. My father walked out of the church toward me, lighting a cigarette and eyeing me silently. There was something about his calmness while I was screaming on the inside that tipped me into running over to him and screaming on the outside. It was almost as if I was outside of myself, watching a desperate nineteen-year-old girl beg her father to do something, say something, fix something. I felt myself return to my body as I started to cry, the cold air in my lungs as I gasped for breath in between sobs. My dad was quietly smoking, looking at his feet.

"Dad," I said, my voice broken, "what are we doing here?" He raised his head, eyes closed, exhaling smoke, and said, "Maybe it's best that you're not here." He turned to go back inside. "Dad," I cried out as he walked away. He ignored me, opening the door. "Dad," I cried out again. "Please don't go," I said again, tears freezing onto my cheeks. He entered the church and the door closed behind him.

Guilt and Shame

I made my way back to my new home and sat on the kitchen floor alone, enveloped in shame about Jesse and Abe, Paul's recriminations reverberating through me. Looking around, I saw that Paul was right. There was minimal artwork on the walls, no toys scattered around, and no fridge full of juice boxes or cut-up veggies. It was a bare-bones townhouse with a few books and toys for the kids. I could hear Adam's voice, signaling me to get curious about why I was choosing this perspective, the viewpoint that I was bad instead of in transition and preparing a life for the kids and myself. I tried it his way, letting the feelings of shame come up and shift, and integrating adaptive information: scenes of me and the kids enjoying the park, me picking up fresh produce daily to cook them healthy meals in the kitchen, me reading them bedtime stories in the night. It seemed to be working—until my mind flashed to the office and how happy I was to be building my own practice. Replacing the positive feelings was a wave of shame at choosing my career over my family. The sensation sunk me. I eyed the fridge, knowing there was a bottle of wine and a tub of ice cream in the freezer. Thankfully,

I had the sense to know that would lead to nowhere good. I grabbed my yoga mat and headed out the door.

The law requires a one-year waiting period after the separation date to file for divorce. I was told this time frame was to allow couples the opportunity to reconcile, something that was not going to be the case for Paul and me. He had been relatively quiet the first few months of our separation, so it was strange that, as we were approaching a year, he was now writing to me that my parents had been "negligent and abusive" with my siblings, and that I was putting our children in "danger" by allowing my parents to visit them once a month.

Ever since I moved into my own home, my parents and I had begun building back our relationship. The work with Adam had helped as my body felt calmer when I was around them, and I was able to articulate my boundaries and expectations. It also helped that my mother was relishing her role as grandmother and didn't want to jeopardize her relationship with me and not see the kids. I was impressed by how great she was with them and how much they loved being with her. I was also surprised by my dad, who was the most present I had ever seen him, teasing the kids and saying "Hello, germs" when he greeted them.

I didn't have any of the safety concerns Paul had about the past. When my grandmother had died years before, my mother's compulsion and desperation to be accepted by the broader family had dissipated. Mom had come to realize how unhealthy her attachments and decisions had been, and had been dedicating time to herself and her own wellness.

Overall, the arrangement was working for the kids, my parents, and me. It was working for everyone except Paul. I was about to experience the full extent of his fear.

Great, Another War

Paul was sending emails arguing about various sections of our parenting agreement. Then I received one titled "Another Safety Issue You Caused," concerning the day after a concert at the boys' school, copied to his lawyer. At the concert, I had steered clear of Paul and stood awkwardly with the other divorced parents, forming our own little circle adjacent to the couples. Like every school concert before, this one was followed by a potluck dinner out in the schoolyard. Abe and I had followed some of his friends and their parents, and Jesse and Paul hung back. I had thought Paul had seen us walk outside, but a few minutes later, he confronted me in the pizza line, accusing me of disappearing with Abe on the day he was responsible for the boys. We were staring at each other, nose to nose, but this time I didn't feel fear or confusion. I felt outrage and I felt my fists ball up. Before I could speak, Jesse reached out and grabbed my hand and grabbed Paul's, smiling his sweet smile, trying to pull us together. We pushed him backward, releasing our hands and walking away from each other. I left the schoolyard without saying goodbye to the children, without saying anything to anyone. I went home, locked the door behind me, and paced my bedroom floor so intensely I could have worn a path in the hardwood. I let every murderous thought race across my mind until they slowed and I cooled down. I got in the shower. I didn't understand why this was happening. It was over, the marriage was over, the divorce over, the division of assets over. I sat down in the tub and let the water thunder against my back while I hugged my knees, watching the water and my tears circle the drain.

After the shower, I went to my computer and forwarded the emails to Susan and scheduled a call with her. "Are you going to be ready to stop this soon?" she asked when we spoke.

"What?" I asked.

"Listen, you and Paul have an abusive dynamic, and neither of you is aware of how you create it together. I'm aware you have a family trauma history, and you have continued your role and position with Paul, and he has continued his." She said this quickly and matter of factly.

"I know," I replied. "We can't seem to break out of it."

"Yes, these patterns are addictive, but at least you have insight. Paul does not, none. You are the one who is going to have to implement changes and put a stop to this. Quite frankly, I've never met a man that wants this much contact with his ex-wife," she said. "I'm sending you to mediation. I have someone good; she's a social worker like you and has seen this before. She'll know how to pull you two apart and set some boundaries."

I exhaled for what felt like the first time that day.

"I've been terrible, too—made things worse," I said, feeling like she mustn't understand the whole story.

"That's your trauma speaking," she said to me, dismissing my statement. "Now about the kids. Research shows that children need one Good Parent and one Good Enough Parent. You are a

Good Parent, and fortunately for all of you so is Paul, or at the least he is a Good Enough Parent."

I knew she was right, but I didn't want to sit across from Paul in mediation. "He'll come around," I argued. "It will be fine."

"Don't make this harder for yourself," Susan said.

———

To my surprise, Paul jumped at the chance for mediation. The day of our appointment, we ended up arriving at the same time, with him carrying what looked like folders and printed copies of our text exchanges. My brother had suggested I do the same, but I couldn't stomach it. I couldn't bear to go over the history, as I wanted to move on, move forward. "Suit yourself," my brother had said. "Just know, you're in a war." *Great, another war*, I thought. I flashed to the image of me sitting on Adam's floor cradling my legs and crying into my knees. *I don't want to fight but there's no choice.*

The mediator met with each of us separately and then brought us together to finalize the amended agreement. In my one-on-one with the mediator, she told me to get myself some support and focused the rest of our meeting on the children. She echoed what I knew, that boundaries and structure promoted safety and security in children, but she added that it was intrusive to have Paul contacting the children every day, that it served the parent's need and not the children's. She also assured me that kids are inherently resilient and adaptive—that they have to be to navigate their environments, as they have no power or control at such a young age. She recommended we shift our parenting schedule from 2-2-3 to 2-2-5, explaining that when kids are going back and forth between households, they need space from the other parent to adapt to the other home and environment, and that the kids needed more time away from each of us and away from our dynamic. She also recommended we use OurFamilyWizard, an app to track our contacts with each other. I agreed to all of it, grateful someone was focused on the children and their well-being separate from our parental chaos. When we met together with Paul, he spent the time focused on his concerns about my parents having access to the kids. The mediator stated she had no concerns at this time, having asked me questions about my parents privately and trusting my judgment. She did however tell Paul he was free to contact child services should he continue to have concerns. He looked frustrated and angry as he left. Alone in the room, I exhaled slowly and rested my head on the table.

Deep Dive

Things remained rocky with Paul even with the app and amended schedule. I got the same number of texts and emails a day, but now they all landed in one place, and I was only required to check it once a day. Even though the change in schedule with the boys helped, the five days together leading to a slower pace and allowing us time to settle into a rhythm, I was feeling the weight of isolation. I wanted human contact, a relationship, or even just a date, but I also didn't want to be in the world of playdates and small talk. It exhausted me to socialize superficially, but I didn't want to be open and let anyone in either. I was stuck.

Miraculously, I was still able to work and be with the kids, but when I wasn't performing my duties, something had shifted in me. I felt I was barely functional in my own time, falling to my knees in tears when I was home alone or dragging myself to yoga where I spent most of the practice crying quietly on my mat in child's pose. This had gone on for a few weeks by the time my brother came to visit.

The kids were with Paul, and I had been sitting at my kitchen table since I got home from work and weeping. When my brother walked in and saw me, he looked shocked. As he sat down, I began bawling uncontrollably about my life, a separated single mother who didn't interact with anyone but her clients, helping them navigate their lives and then coming home to cry alone, missing her kids, and scared for the future, believing she had made a massive mistake in destroying her family.

My brother looked at me with frustration. Ever since he returned from a yoga retreat in Portugal, he was different. And it wasn't all the weight he had shed, what he described as *psychic and physical baggage*. It was his whole outlook on life. As I sat there feeling sorry for myself, he pushed the table away from him and stood up. "God, Natasha, look at you, sitting there crying over a life that didn't fit you and wasn't meant for you," he said. "Do you know who you are?" he continued. "You're like the girl with a rosemary ham tucked under her arm sitting there crying because she doesn't have a crust of bread."

I buried my head in my hands as he walked out the door. I could feel the truth of his words but I couldn't get there. I couldn't get to the truth tucked right under my arm. All I saw was the crusts of bread crumbling all around me while I starved.

———

"You need a deep dive," Adam said to me, looking concerned about my mental and physical health. By then I was rail thin, and I knew I looked sickly. I sat, defeated, on his couch. I had been canceling my appointments with Adam and avoiding everything in my life other than work and looking after the kids. I was able to focus on my clients, and my decade of experience and love for the work kept me engaged and functional in that context. With the kids, I could keep my attention on cooking and lunch packing, and they seemed happy to have more screen time while I locked myself away in the bathroom to cry in the shower. I knew I needed help. Sitting there in front of Adam it was confirmed: I was in trouble. He told me about a place called Ryzio in Arizona that would provide me with the healing support I needed, that a few sessions a month with him was not enough, and that I needed a retreat setting. He explained that the amount of fear and trauma embedded in my nervous system was considerable and a reset was required. I nodded. I couldn't live like this anymore.

CHAPTER V

Approaching the Innermost Cave

The Retreat

A month after an exploratory phone call with the Ryzio program director, Dr. Marti Glenn, I was on a plane to Arizona. I was traveling with a broken spirit and a body in need of healing. I required the will to save myself. It seemed I had it, just barely.

I arrived at the most magnificent ranch, where the retreat was being held, and my room was beautiful. It had a gas fireplace and big bathtub. It also had a back door that led to the desert, dotted with massive cacti and exotic plants. At my front door was an orange tree with little green and yellow oranges hanging from it. I sat on the bed. I missed Jesse. I missed Abe. I even missed Paul. It felt like so much had happened in such a short time and it all felt like it had happened to me, and was not caused by me. It was time to go to "circle," which was the first thing listed on the itinerary. I wiped my tears, threw my hair in a ponytail, and grabbed the paper map, hoping I could navigate to where I needed to be.

As I walked out the door, I was shoulder to shoulder to a man who had just left his room and was busily locking his door.

"Hello," I said as I locked my own door.

"Hi, I'm Ben," came the reply. "You here for Ryzio?" I liked the feel of him.

"I am. Not really sure what to expect, but I'm here," I admitted.

"Well, I'm sure you're in the right place," he said kindly. "This is my second time in about seven years, and the first time changed my life."

I was comfortable and centered walking through the ranch, smiling and chatting with Ben as he guided me through the property. I felt Ben was my security blanket, and I ignored the pesky voice in my head that chastised me for always having a man to stitch my safety to. As we entered the large room, my security blanket quickly left me and began to greet and hug people milling around, and I stood in the doorway wanting to flee. He ended up sitting across from me in a group of sixteen people and another four staff members. I looked around the room and saw a dark-haired, beautiful woman looking hostile and wrapped in cashmere perched on a yoga bolster. Two men were adjacent to her, one older, wearing glasses, tall and neat, legs crossed, and the other guy sprawled on the floor, picking at lint in the carpet, looking bored. I overhead his name was Mark, and the three of them were all from Ontario, Canada, like me. I scanned the rest of the circle and was unimpressed by the middle-aged group assembled there. I was clearly the youngest but hopefully not the most screwed up.

"Why hello, dear one," came a singsong voice in my direction, "I'm so glad you made it." It was Marti. I instantly relaxed, as though a loving mother was excited to have me home from school.

"Hi, Marti," I said, surprised to hear my voice crack.

"It's so good to meet you in person. You're here," she said with what seemed like genuine happiness. She lightly touched my arm and brought me to the circle, introducing me to the person on my left and right as "Natasha from Toronto." I said hello to "Angela from California" and "Christy from South Dakota."

Before I became too uncomfortable with small talk, a gong-like bell sounded and a petite man in his late sixties moved to the middle of the circle, holding one of those sound bowls I'd seen in gift shops. "Hello, everyone," he said. "I'd like us to take our seats so we can begin." Christy smiled at me, and awkwardly I smiled back. "I'm Ken," continued the man with the sound bowl, "and Marti and I are so happy to meet you all and have you here." There was something about the way he said this, slowly making eye contact with each of us, that formed a tightness in my stomach and the powerful urge to start crying. *What the hell is wrong with me?* I kept thinking. *Get a hold of yourself.*

I quickly learned that Ken and Marti were married and ran this program together, their life's work. After they introduced themselves and the two coaches, Jamie and Sherry, they opened up the circle to our group to introduce ourselves. We were asked to share our name, where we were from, and our passion. *Ugghh*, I thought. The beautiful brunette was named Bianca and she didn't know what her passion was. I liked her a little more as she said that. When it was my turn, my voice wavered. I struggled to announce that my passion was my children, the safe answer but not the honest one. Like Bianca, I had no idea what my passion was. Surviving had been my dedication, but I'm not sure you also get a passion with that. I spent the rest of the circle time fearing I had made a huge mistake and wanting to run out the door and go back to my beautiful room with the orange tree out front.

Safety

It was the first morning, and we were all sitting like children around the circle again. Marti greeted us and conducted a morning check-in. "Who knows what safety means?" she asked. Christy spoke up quickly: "That I'm free from harm." Something was different about her face. She looked ten years older than the day before. I realized she didn't have an ounce of makeup on, and she looked as if she had spent the night crying. She was sitting next to Bianca, who looked as beautiful and perfect as yesterday.

"That's right, Christy." Marti sent her a warm smile. "It means I'm free from harm, and we're going to talk about what harm is. Any other examples of safety?"

I was gearing up for a discussion on abuse and violence when Ben, my neighbor with the orange trees, raised his hand and said, "Safety means *all of me can be here.*"

"Thank you, Ben," said Ken. "You got it: All of me can be here." I hadn't heard that before.

The next hour or so, Marti and Ken spoke of the latest neuroscience in the fields of attachment, epigenetics, and polyvagal theory. I was familiar with attachment theory, it being the backbone of my practice, but I appreciated the addition of epigenetics and the understanding of nature and nurture instead of the argument of nature *versus* nurture. They began by referencing Dr. Daniel Siegel, the emerging expert in studying attachment on the brain, quoting that early experience shapes the structure and function of the brain, which reveals the fundamental way in which gene expression is determined by experience. Marti, who was a leader in the field of perinatal and prenatal mental health, explained that early life experiences set our hard wiring and the lens with which we would experience the world in adulthood, such as the trauma in our relationships. It was as if our young, developing brains were *programmed* to experience and interact with the world in certain ways.

Marti and Ken gave some concrete examples. Young children with nurturing and attuned adults in their lives, they said, had a built-in program that the world was good, people were kind, and they had the competency and ability to achieve their goals and ask for help. These individuals responded to the world with trust and ability to give and receive. In contrast, if your early life experiences and attachments taught you can't trust others, others are dangerous, you would most likely develop a program that responds and reacts to the world with mistrust, manipulation, control, doubt, or fear. Marti and Ken explained that the program operates unconsciously, scanning the environment and picking out information that confirms the painful, unresolved life experiences of your past. This program then generates the automatic responses that kept you safe in the past. However, reactions like mistrust and control, which were once adaptive in your childhood environment, are maladaptive in your adult world.

I thought about some of my own clients, one of them a lovely man who was seeing me about self-esteem and depression. He had an alcoholic mother and had learned to stay out of her way as a child. Unfortunately, the strategy worked too well with his aggressive wife and incompetent boss and his ability to make empowered choices for himself. I was taking notes, writing furiously how the various parts of the brain and neural pathways activated the unconscious programming. Ken was talking about regulating the nervous system, and I was mindful that distracting myself with the educational aspect was a useful strategy for me to avoid feeling the pit in my stomach and the tears that kept threatening to come up every time Marti or Ken made eye contact with me.

Mark spoke out: "But I don't remember anything from before I was five. I don't even remember anything before I was ten. My parents were great. It's not their fault that my life is a mess."

Again, with kindness and care from Marti, she said, "Yes, a lot of us don't have mental memories of our childhood, but our body has the memory of it and our patterns of being show us what early program we were wired with."

I thought about Adam in those early sessions, before I had given him any of my history—how he said he could read my trauma from the way I interacted with the world. I brought my attention back to Marti, who was still addressing Mark. "I agree with you. This is not about blaming our parents or anyone. They couldn't give us what they didn't get, and if they didn't feel safe in their early childhood or didn't get the connections they needed to develop a healthy nervous system, then they couldn't give it to us." Mark nodded and a few other group members relaxed their shoulders. Marti continued: "The great news is that we can rewire our brains, we can update our nervous systems, and we can develop that sense of safety needed to create our lives from a place of presence and wholeness."

For the rest of the morning, Ken and Marti talked about rewiring the nervous system and opening up our *neural nets* to release an *old program* and update it with new patterns of being. I had never heard language like this before, and I allowed myself to feel the tingle gliding up my spine all the way up to the crown of my head. Something was happening there.

———

The rest of the afternoon involved more psychoeducation about boundaries and something called the *drama triangle*. I was whipping through my notebook, filling it with pages and pages of notes and diagrams. I loved the way Marti and Ken explained boundaries, which was "I am only as free to ask as you are free to refuse" and "The wall that keeps you out also imprisons me." And my favorite: "You must have a *no* in order for your *yes* to be meaningful." They explained that boundaries are essential to keep us out of the *drama triangle*, where we take a turn in the role of victim, persecutor, or rescuer in our relationships. I stopped writing. I flashed on how I didn't recognize the need for my own boundaries, and how even if I did, I didn't express my needs. I had the belief that if Paul really loved me, he would see my need; I shouldn't have to tell him. I flashed on how I would give too much, like staying up late with the babies because it suited Paul's schedule even when I was resentful. I realized I was inadvertently putting myself in the victim category. I had done that countless times, made excuses for his behavior, overcompensating and overdoing, which inevitably led to me shifting to the persecutor stance, raging at him for taking advantage of me. And then, after I'd cut him down in my anger, how gallantly I would play the role of rescuer, the therapist ready to put our family life back together. I cringed thinking back to my patterns with Paul, the cycles of our abusiveness. I could see the dynamic between my mother and father even more clearly than my own.

As intrigued as I was about all the education, I was ready to get onto the work. I knew the toxic environment I was born into, had the coherent narrative of all the wrongs done to me, and had catalogued all the people that had wronged me. That is what I had spent half my life in therapy doing. I knew the coping strategies, the self-talk, journaling, observing my thoughts, and naming my emotions. I knew how to take "time outs" and count to ten, and I had tried various rounds of antidepressants over the years. I had spent the other half of my life pursuing my role as a therapist to help other people understand all the trauma that had happened to them.

"We're breaking into our small groups now, and the one you're assigned to will be your group for the rest of the week," Jamie said. Nervous, I scanned the room and worried about whom I would have to share my story with. I caught Marti's eye, and she walked over. She said warmly, "Lucky me. I get to choose my group and I'm so happy you're with me."

I exhaled, surprised that I had been holding my breath. Angela, Christy, and Bianca joined us to make our group of four. Each group wandered off with their coaches, and Marti led the four of us to a private room where there were bolsters, pillows, and blankets arranged in a circle. We sat down and curled up in blankets, giggling about what a sweet group we were, with Marti singing a happy little song that the other women hummed along to. I was happy to be in this little cocoon but singing made me shy, my mother being the first to let me know that singing wasn't one of my gifts.

Wise Adult

"Hello, everyone," Marti addressed us again as we sat down for our first small group the next morning. I looked around at the other three women in the circle with me. I was thinking how much I liked Christy, having sat with her at dinner the night before. There were Kleenex boxes everywhere, one right next to Christy. She nudged it over, nestling it between us. I had tortured myself all night about all the suffering Jesse and Abe would have in their lives because of me. I had worried about my future, how to navigate my business, and how to take care of the boys and my home financially. When I looked at myself in the mirror that morning, I was a mess. Unlike Christy, I smeared on as much makeup as possible to look presentable. In that small circle, sitting next to the Kleenex boxes, I was regretting that choice.

Marti had us all go around the circle, introducing ourselves more intimately than we had with the larger group. This time I volunteered to go first, wanting to get it over with. I shared that I couldn't seem to stop cycling through intense fear and anger, and my life was chaotic with my ex-husband, on top of raising two young kids and managing a business on my own. Christy went next, saying that she was there to save her marriage. She said it was her third, that she felt she had chosen wrong, again, and was there to see if the problem might be her. Angela followed and talked longer than me and Christy combined. Even after all that sharing, I wasn't sure why she was there. She irritated me. She was in her late fifties, was some kind of nebulous academic, and was simultaneously into poetry, philosophy, anti-oppressive theory, neuroscience, and Chinese mysticism. She said a lot and nothing at the same time, but the thing that irritated me the most was that she sounded like my mother when Mom adopted that sweet, syrupy voice to manipulate us. I found myself rolling my eyes a lot when Angela was talking. It was Bianca's turn next. She cleared her throat and said she was attracting sex addicts and bad boys. She explained that she had a high-powered role in a successful family business, but she was often treated like "a little girl who isn't capable." The more she spoke, the less I was drawn to her appearance and the more I felt a warmth and care for her. As she told us what it was like co-parenting with a sex addict (apparently, they always have half-naked women around), I could see past the hair and makeup to a sweet, small girl who wanted to be loved, and I found I wanted to be kind to her. I looked at Christy and felt the same way. I turned my gaze to Angela, but I still didn't have any warmth for her.

Marti thanked us all for sharing and began orienting us to what we would be doing for the day. "We all have a *wise adult* inside of us that is aware, can hold boundaries, make amends as needed, and learn from mistakes. This is the part of us that sees the big picture and can make choices for long-term satisfaction rather than short-term satisfaction." We settled in as she spoke, sprawled out among the pillows, and pulled blankets up to our chins. "This wise adult acts with authenticity and compassion," she continued. "The more we allow this part of us to emerge, the healthier we become. We are working toward having this wise adult be in charge most of the time, helping us grow our window of presence."

She reviewed some of the work from the day before, how our old program, the way we've managed to have our needs met in the past, can be maladaptive given our present circumstances and adult lives. She outlined a few of these strategies, such as manipulation, people pleasing, acquiescing, and fighting, which are *safety strategies* that hijack our nervous systems subconsciously (outside of our awareness) and run our lives. Because it's the same automatic program, we end up with the same outcome: one sex addict after another, or in my case, fighting and fleeing in my relationships.

Marti passed out a few pens, had us open our Ryzio workbooks, and asked us to make a few lists of how we have experienced our wise adult operating in our lives and what it feels like being led by her. Chewing on my pen and thinking, thinking, thinking some more, I drew a blank. I was great at writing when I was copying Marti's genius; however, I didn't seem to have any inside of myself to express on the page. Marti came over to me and asked me to close my eyes and focus on my breath. I did, feeling the tension in my arms relax, the pressured need to "get this right" dissipating. "Now," she said, "visualize your wise adult. What she would sound like, what are the words she would say?" I kept my eyes closed and heard Marti walk away, leaving me with myself. Part of me seemed to have thrown in the towel, saying, *"You don't have one, sis. Sorry, but ain't no wise adult here."* I kept breathing. Then another voice, this one sad, said, *"You've never had a wise adult, never, not one day in your life."* I just kept breathing.

Then an image appeared. I could see myself sitting at the kitchen table of the townhouse; it was dark, the room only lit by the oven light, and I was sitting with my head in my hands, a glass of wine on the table. It was so vivid, and though it was me, it seemed like another version of me—a worn-out, exhausted, and defeated version. I could hear the thoughts in her head, which were on repeat: all the ways I had tormented myself last night. I kept focused on this image, watching it like a movie. Then I saw a figure standing next to this version of me, one that felt kind and loving even though I couldn't make out the image. I kept my eyes on it. The more I relaxed the clearer the image became. It was Marti, my wise adult!

The wise adult Marti put her hands gently on the shoulders of that version of me and said, "It's going to be all right, dear one. You're not alone. You are doing the best you can, making choices each day with the best intentions for you and your children. It will be all right. Be kind to yourself. I love you." I felt touched at this gentleness. I felt peace, and tears slowly slid down my cheeks. The tears had rolled to my chin when I heard a voice in my head call me a *loser* and *idiot*, that I had to borrow a wise adult from a woman whom I was paying, that I didn't even have my own. I put my cap back on my pen and closed my empty notebook, waiting for the exercise to end.

Small Group

The small group was the pinnacle of Ryzio. Bianca, Angela, Christy, and I held space and each other as Marti led us into our bodies to follow and release the memories, pain, and experiences we embedded in our subconscious. It was the same work I was doing with Adam, which made sense considering he had been a student of Marti and Ken, but there was something about a group of people loving you through your pain that was transformational. Each of us took a turn with Marti as the rest sat in support, and I was awed once again by the power of this process when Bianca was in the middle of the group for her turn. I was sitting behind her, back-to-back, so she could physically feel that someone had her back as she followed the tight knots in her stomach. She wept, first quietly and then loudly as she shared aloud the flood of images of her ex-husband and male family members berating her and putting her down. Marti had reiterated what Adam had taught me: that by allowing the experience and pain to surface, it could be witnessed, acknowledged, and released. With Marti's experienced guidance, Bianca let go of the past so she could be present to create her future. Bianca was looking around the room, at Christy and Angela's caring faces. She was updating her body. The past was over, and she was experiencing safety, no judgment. She could be the messy, imperfect human she was and still be loved.

One by one, we took turns through those next few days, each of us feeling more vulnerable and more able to expose the pain and shame we had buried. I even warmed to Angela; the more her know-it-all exterior safety strategy dissolved, the more real she was. She had relaxed into a quiet and thoughtful person. Even her voice changed. I was changing, too. I sat in the middle of the circle during my turn with no words, just tears, and rather than push them away, I let these four beautiful women sit around me like guardian angels blanketing me with love and peace. Silence was the most beautiful gift.

Arts and Crafts

Every day also included craft time, which we did as a large group. All sixteen of us piled into a room with stacks and stacks of magazines and art supplies, and we were invited to make collages representing our internal worlds and choose pictures that depicted *parts* of ourselves. I was lost. Several different images registered but didn't seem cohesive. I distracted myself by watching what others were doing. In the first few days, I saw Bianca busily ripping out pictures of high fashion and starving models juxtaposed with dominant, powerful men. I looked over at Mark, who was busy giggling to himself, pasting pictures of cool bands on his board. It was an interesting exercise to see people express themselves despite how cheesy it sounded for a group of grown-ups to pay thousands of dollars to craft. Slowly, my board took shape as I stopped second-guessing my choices and pulled and pasted whatever resonated with me. Soon, I was astounded to see the themes represented on my board. They were all different images and ages, but what they had in common was fierceness and fear. There were tough girls and women with fists, sneers, determined looks, and hardship. It felt accurate, and it felt exhausting.

Over the next few days of therapy and group work, we would go back to the craft room, and it was amazing to see how our daily creations were shifting. We were all evolving yet staying true to who we were. Bianca still had pretty women on her boards, yet they were less dominated by men. There were more pictures of reading in the sunshine, pretty pastel sweaters, and other images of comfortable clothes and loose ponytails.

My own board was evolving from images of defiant independence to fragility and smallness. I had pictures of young girls wearing outfits too grown up for them, posing for the camera like scared rabbits. Pictures of girls and women hiding behind doors, walls, and books. And I was crying more, a lot more, which I didn't think was possible. Marti said it was because I had "a lot of tears to make up for," and that it was now safe for my body to start letting them out. I didn't know if that was true, but I knew that every act of kindness that came my way made me tear up, like when Mark, whom I had misjudged and who had become like a protective older brother to me, told me he looked forward to seeing me in circle because I always had such interesting insights. Or when Ben said that one of his favorite parts of the day was our quiet walks back to the room after dinner, where we didn't have to say a word to each other but enjoyed each other's silent company. Sherry would find me on one of her daily walks, lying against a big, ancient tree out in the desert, looking up at the mountains. She would give me a warm look and tell me what a highlight it was for her to come across such a smile.

Normally, this type of positivity and kindness would make me suspicious and uncomfortable, like "What do you want from me?" and

"What's the angle?" But there it felt good and, most importantly, authentic. I felt the same way about these people. I loved seeing them in circle, out on a walk, or down by the ranch. It was always an unexpected treat. For the first time in my life outside of my office, I genuinely wanted to be around people. I wanted to connect and enjoy others' company.

————

"If you let your mind float back, just let it go. What experience comes up when you think about trust and feel safe to have someone care for you?" This was the question being asked in our large group. I closed my eyes, and nothing came up. Nothing. I sat for a while, focusing on my breath. I told that to Marti as she came by. She told me to follow my body instead of my thoughts, to feel the sensations and see where they would lead me.

We were sent off with our workbooks and instructed to link current situations in our lives with sensations in our bodies and allow memories of some of the earliest situations in our histories to come up, then write them down. I found a special tree out in an area beyond the ranch that was quiet and barren; it felt good there. I thought about the end of my marriage, the current state of push and pull for control. For this exercise, I practiced "noticing what I noticed," which was the tension in my body. I focused my attention on the sensations, curious toward the emotion of anger deep in my chest, as if it was pumping adrenaline. It fascinated me that even though I could be sitting in the middle of nowhere with no threat to my safety, my thoughts of attachment safety could trigger enough cortisol in my body to fight off a lion. I kept watching from this wise adult place and could feel this pressure in my chest and restlessness in my legs, as if I had to act, had to run. It then seemed to shift away from pressure to a dropping sensation. In fact, it felt as if the ground had been taken out from under me and I was falling. When I landed, I was in a pit of sadness. I was hollow on the inside and way down deep was a sadness I didn't know was there. It shifted again, and this time I was gripped by intense fear. I observed the fear, watched it creep up from my legs, into my torso, chest, neck, arms, and hands. A small voice in my head said I'd be good, I'd be better, promised not to be so challenging, so difficult. What had become terror began to dissipate and I was left with the emotion of disgust. I was revolted at myself for being in such vulnerability, such need. This was too much. I winced and opened my eyes. Experiment over.

I Used to Date You

I was the first to leave for lunch, not wanting to share my experience of the exercise and realizing I was starving. On my way to the dining room, I decided I didn't want to sit with anyone, so I quietly got a plate from the buffet and looked down at my feet, knowing others would think I was deep in meditation or reflection and not bother me. But Ben showed up. "Hey, was wondering where you ran off to," he said.

"Oh, me? Yeah, lots of thinking and journaling. I'm going to have a reflective lunch and be with myself," I said, walking away.

He followed me with his plate. "Cool, me also. Let's sit together and practice stillness and being with ourselves together," he said with a smile. My initial reaction was to tell him off: *Have you learned nothing about boundaries?!* Instead, I kept moving, thinking maybe he was joking. I sat down and began to eat my roast beef and pasta salad, keeping my head down. Ben ate a crunchy apple across from me, looking right at me, and I ignored him. He kept crunching for a time and then said, "I used to date you."

I felt the anger in my fists and the *fuck you* on the tip of my tongue. I was goddamn sick and tired of being made to feel uncomfortable. I cursed my mother for teaching me how to be pleasant when I wanted to be rude. I cursed myself for not being able to set a boundary.

"Yeah, I dated you seven years ago," he continued, ignorant to my discomfort. "Her name was Sarah, and she was beautiful, funny, amazingly smart, and could light up a room," he smiled, lost in the memory. "She was also confusing as hell, always finding herself in some crisis and fighting her way through or running the other way only to yo-yo back to me." He had my attention. "It was exhausting being with her, but I loved her so much. Still do," he said, swallowing.

"What happened to her?" I asked

"She's still running around in crisis, jumping around her drama triangle, believing the whole world is against her. Don't get me wrong—she got dealt a bad hand. Her mama was always suicidal, and her dad ran out on them when she was young. A few of her stepdads had a go at her, too. It was a mess. When I met her, I was drawn to her fierce independence coupled with her deep vulnerability. It was like kryptonite," he said and stopped eating, looking down, talking to himself more so than me.

"So, what happened with you two?"

"I got sick of it, sick of the drama and the fighting and the loving and the running and the hating. It was like being on a merry-go-round, and I didn't like who I was becoming. I was a real asshole to her, cheating on her when she pushed me away and ignoring her when she kept coming back."

We were interrupted by Christy, who had appeared smiling and hoping to join us. Ben looked at her and said, "Sorry, my dear. We're having a private conversation. Hope to sit with you at dinner." Christy looked crushed but walked away.

I was fascinated that Ben did that so easily, so politely, and so completely unconcerned with how it impacted Christy. He looked at me. "She's a grown-up. She can figure out where to sit and handle her own feelings about it."

I loved that concept. People are grown-ups who can figure it out. It was so simple, and I wanted it to be true, but watching Christy hang her head and walk away, I wasn't so sure.

"Anyway, as I was saying," Ben continued, "it was the experience with Sarah that made me stop and look at my behavior, not just what I felt she was turning me into. That's when I first met Marti and Ken." He returned to crunching his apple. "That experience with Sarah was a gift. I saw how she wasn't the first woman I tried to rescue and ended up punishing. It's my program, my pattern, and she was just playing her part in my story."

The words hit me, the truth of that sunk in, and I could feel a tingle running up my spine and a shiver at the back of my neck, like a signal that those words were for me. "So," he said, "what character do you play for other people, and what do they play for you?" I excused myself, telling Ben what he shared was useful, but I had to go journal. He sat mouth open. I smiled and said, "You're a grown-up. You'll be fine."

He laughed. "Yeah, I dated you all right."

All Is Forgiven, Move On

The next morning, back again in our large group, eight of us formed a large circle, and the other eight group members formed a smaller circle on the inside. I was part of the outside circle, standing in front of a woman named Vanessa, who was on the inside. Marti told us we were going to take turns singing to each other, then the outside circle was going to shift around so that we would be standing in front of a new person. My hands were getting clammy. I did not want to sing. But I'm a good student and trusted Marti; so, I stood there making "brief and frequent" eye contact with Vanessa, which I had learned would help grow my vagus nerve and reduce the chance of me getting hijacked into my old program of reacting. Marti had been teaching us about the vagus nerve, describing it as the CEO of our nervous system and primarily responsible for keeping us in "rest and digest mode." I had learned about the two branches of the nervous system and how staying in the parasympathetic nervous system allows my body to be consciously present, with my immune system and other vital systems working optimally. As the exercise began, I looked into Vanessa's eyes and felt ease in singing to her in harmony with Marti and eight other voices: "All is forgiven, move on."

Then it was my turn to receive, to have Vanessa look at me and sing, "All is forgiven, move on." *There was no way I could do this.* No way I could walk around this circle and have eight people look into my eyes and tell me I was forgiven, that I was good, that I was free to forgive myself and move on. But there she was, Vanessa, holding my shoulders, looking at me tenderly and singing into my heart, "All is forgiven, move on." It was as if a violent wave was crashing through me from the inside. I was weak in the knees and not sure I could hold myself up much longer. I shook and shook with these loving words, my eyes squeezed tight, not able to look at her. But I had to open my eyes—being in the outside circle, I had to shift to my right and the person next to me and repeat.

Thankfully, the next person was Christy, and I trusted Christy. I grasped her shoulders, and as I opened my mouth to sing to her, I felt a strength in my arms and a clarity in my voice as I looked deeply into her eyes and sang to her. But again, as Christy touched my shoulders and lovingly sang the words to me, I shook and sobbed. Each time, round and round the circle, feelings of grief, relief, and release took me over.

But by the fifth person, it no longer felt like me singing to my group or them singing to me; instead, it felt like a divine force cleansing all the sins of my heart, as if God was singing to me that I was forgiven, that I could move on. I also knew in my heart that if I held onto this shame, guilt, and grief, I couldn't be available to my kids, I couldn't serve my clients, and I couldn't enjoy the bounty of love and experiences of the world that lay before me like a gift. The eighth and final person in front of me was Edward. In the group, Edward kept mostly to himself, a tall and elegant man who had been the last to arrive. He was wealthy and ran a large international corporation, often busy on his cellphone during the breaks. I hadn't spoken to him the whole week we'd been there, and our lives felt miles apart. As I stood before him, I felt stronger and softer simultaneously, all the forgiveness and love I'd been granted so far buoying me. Edward looked me in the eyes as I gazed up at him. As he began singing to me, he became tearful, and I watched him struggle to maintain eye contact with me. Witnessing his pain, I felt an immediate call to provide stability, steadiness, and peace. I reached up and rested my hand on his upper arm, not able to reach his shoulder. I looked in his eyes and sang as he wept and wept, gripping my shoulders as if I was keeping him upright. There we were, two people miles apart and yet together, holding each other, singing love and peace directly into the other's heart.

———

Back in my room, sitting alone in front of the fireplace, I closed my eyes and could feel an openness and a heat in my chest that startled me. Putting the Ryzio tools into practice, I noticed the sensation and linked it to the feelings of love and openness I experienced when looking at Jesse and Abe. I then thought about the quiet teas I would have with James, the cigar chats with Trevor, my blossoming friendship with the beautiful Bianca, and the sharing with Ben and everyone's kindness toward me. I realized that maybe I was the kind, good person they told me I was, the woman they reflected back to me, and that I was making a contribution to people around me. I was in some small way making people feel good just by Being.

It was so strange to think that way. I knew when I was a therapist that I was helping people with my effort, knowledge, and skill. I knew when I was taking care of the boys, I was being a good mother with my effort, energy, and time. But at Ryzio, I was focused on myself. How was that adding value? I thought about it a little more and realized I was genuinely present in a way I hadn't been with most people. I felt warmth toward all the other participants, even Angela, and paid attention to their sharing time because I cared about them, not just because it was polite. I was *Being* and the response I was receiving was love and kindness.

Meant to Be Here

It was time for an individual process with Marti and Ken—one that would, as they said, explore my *earliest experience*. I wasn't sure what we would be doing, because even though everyone had their own time with Marti and Ken, none of them described the experience. But I noticed how differently they carried themselves afterward. It was as if they were slower, calmer, and more present. I walked into the bigger room, where Marti and Ken were set up in the corner with blankets and pillows. The lights were dim and the space quiet.

"Hello, dear one," said Marti when she spotted me. Ken gave me a warm hug. I could hear a small, skeptical voice in the back of my head, unsure what we would be doing. But it quickly subsided— there was a knowing, a belief in these two people. Their authenticity and dedication to true healing shone through.

"I'm a little nervous about what this is," I said.

"Yes, that makes sense," came Marti's reply. "It's important we're oriented to what we're doing and why in order to feel safe."

She explained that our birth and any trauma associated with the experience is imprinted in our cells, that our bodies carry this earliest of experiences. She cited studies about the impact of cesarean sections and other medically assisted births on the child, effects that carry over into the adult life. None of this was judgmental or political, just fact and research based, and today's process was an opportunity to allow the body and the initial imprint to heal. I trusted them, and importantly, I was trusting myself to experience the process, to take any value for me and leave the rest behind.

Marti and Ken invited me to sit on the blankets, and we had an easy chat about how I was feeling at Ryzio. I took notice of how quiet I was when I was with them, how gentle I was. I wished I was more like this with my boys. It would be good for Abe and Jesse to have such a relaxed and soft mother. I shared these reflections with Marti and Ken.

"This is who you are," Marti said to me, looking into my eyes and nodding. "This is you when you feel safe, this is who we are when we're safe." I thought of how this applied to the people in my life. To Paul, and the softness, kindness, and gentleness I received from him throughout our dating, marriage, and life together when he felt he could be himself, safe, and accepted. I thought of my mother and my father and when they were safe, how wonderful it was to have them at my volleyball games, school concerts, and graduations. Yes, when they felt safe in their own bodies, in their own life, they were loving, warm, and caring. Those thoughts quickly melted away, though, and the abuse, anger, and resentment resurfaced.

"Notice what you notice," said Ken, attuned to my internal shifts.

"I guess I'm noticing how quickly I move from good thoughts and feelings to bad ones," I said.

"Yes," said Marti. "You have strong protectors, which isn't a bad thing, but it's a hard thing when they are from our old program and have little bearing on the lives we live today. You were programmed early. We all were. Let's see what that was for you when you were born."

The instructions were simple: "Notice what you notice and follow your body." I lay silently on the blanket, initially self-conscious about Ken and Marti watching me as I lay there. I noticed the thoughts in my mind; they quickly subsided. And I noticed that I felt uncomfortable the way I was laying; I wanted to be on all fours.

I moved my body into child's pose, wrapping my arms over my head. That felt nice. When I was a bundled ball, Marti put a blanket over me, and I was cocooned as if in a womb. Briefly, I thought, *This is bullshit*, and it felt a little hokey, but again I was able to let those thoughts melt away, to stay with the process. My body seemed to want to sway. I moved side to side and back and forth, and it felt right, it felt good. I then wanted to roll up more tightly and have the blanket cover my head. Without words, I felt Marti and Ken tuck the blankets around and under me, tightly wrapping me into a safe little mound.

All the muscles in my body relaxed and my mind quieted. It was quiet everywhere. I stayed like this for what felt like a long time, indulging in the choice to be as I was and not worry about taking up Marti and Ken's time or worry if I was doing it right. Then something deep inside me stirred, wanted to move. I began to sway again, side to side, then back and forth again. It was hot, it was cramped; I didn't want to be in there anymore. As I made a move to stretch out, I felt fear, yet I didn't want to not be in there either. It was confusing, wanting the peace and stillness of inside but feeling cramped and tight and wanting the freedom of outside. I stayed where I was, hoping the urge to go out would go away so I could stay in. But it came again, this time stronger, and the thought came that I wanted to be with Marti and Ken, wanted to be with the group and out in the world. I started toward the opening of the blanket, seeking air. As I emerged, I could feel Marti and Ken on the outside, slowly and expertly following my movements. Then I heard them singing and I wanted to get out from under, to be with them and their love.

My hands were the first thing to come through the opening and then I stopped, a tug in my belly and a fear in my heart. It was too late to stay. I was out and had to continue out, knowing I couldn't stay in there forever. As I pushed to get free of these tight blankets and pillows, I could feel Marti reach in and pull me out and into her lap because I didn't have the energy to crawl out on my own. Deep sadness and the longing to go back in crashed over me. Marti held me to her chest and stroked my hair, allowing me to weep and take in gulps of air while she rocked me back and forth.

"You are my sunshine, my only sunshine, you make me happy when skies are gray," she sang. "You'll never know, dear, how much I love you, please don't take, my sunshine away."

Ken finished the song. "You are my sunshine, my only sunshine," they sang together. "You make me happy, when skies are gray," they continued. As they sang, Marti rocked me and Ken came closer, keeping a distance but staying nearer to us, singing sweetly. I allowed myself to be rocked, cradled, loved. While they were doing this, images came up of my mother and father, young, in their twenties. I could see my father looking at my mother, my mother looking at my father as she held me, a baby. In that moment, they loved me. In that moment, they wanted me. I felt my chest open up and a tingling run up and down my arms and legs. I was wanted. I was loved. I was meant to be here.

PART II

DESTINY

CHAPTER VI

Descent

It was time to go home, back to Toronto and back to my life. Marti and Ken hosted a beautiful closing ceremony, and we were invited to sit in the middle of the circle and share our truth about who we were, not what our old program dictated. Nine days earlier, this exercise would have angered me, would have felt syrupy, too sappy. But on that day I sat tall and straight, filled with confidence and grace for myself with these beautiful souls around me. One by one, people shared what they were taking away from the week, and I realized how much work everyone had done in their small groups, that we were leaving so different from how we arrived, more our true selves. Mark was the last to go; he had emerged from this last week at Ryzio as an important member of our group. When women in the group were sharing their experiences of toxic masculinity in their lives, I intuitively looked to Mark for balance. In Mark, I had experienced what I considered heroic masculinity. When I was feeling vulnerable, I felt safety and strength in his strong, protective hug. When I was feeling sad and alone, he was kind, and gentle with his listening. When I was feeling unsteady and unsure in the group, I knew to look at him and make eye contact. As we sat there at the end of the retreat, he was sitting in the middle of the group. Taking a moment to look around and make eye contact with each one of us, he said, "I really want to thank everyone who was here. I mean that. You're all good people, and I appreciate every one of you. I've done a lot of stuff before and a lot of programs, and I hope this sticks."

We nodded, all of us hoping "this sticks." As we headed back to our rooms to get our bags and board shuttle buses for the airport, Ben gave me a big hug and handed me an orange from our tree. "It was a special week. I learned a lot from you," he said with a smile. He put his hands on my shoulders and looked me in the eyes and said, "You are perfect. You are the most perfect Natasha, just as you are."

Internal Family Systems

For the next few months, I practiced being mindful, noticing the sensations in my body and the thoughts in my head. It was a lot of work and I realized how much more slowly I needed my life to be to remain conscious of all the ways my mind and body were interacting with the world. I had become a walking billboard for Ryzio and told everyone I could about it. I kept in touch with Bianca and Mark, and we continued supporting and encouraging each other back in our real lives. Even with a full work schedule, I found myself more relaxed with everyone, especially Jesse and Abe, and I felt less like I was caregiving for them and more like I was caring for them, enjoying their company. I was also meditating regularly, journaling, and eating grapefruits every morning. I was changing and so was my life.

My clients were also responding to Marti and Ken's teachings, which I had brought into my practice, and soon I had a waitlist forming. Even though I had far more autonomy in my private practice, and I felt more energized with clients practicing from more of a Ryzio model, I still often felt burned out and drained, like I was pushing my clients up a hill toward their healing rather than walking alongside them in their journey. Over the years I had been told by different supervisors that I was "doing too much" and was reminded of the therapist adage: "Don't work harder than your clients."

I had continued learning more about the nervous system after coming home from Arizona, researching some of the leaders in the field that Marti had referenced, such as doctors Daniel Siegel, Stephen Porges, Alan Schore, and Peter Levine. I liked their work, which resonated with me and felt true. One day, while sitting at my desk and returning emails, I received a forwarded message from a therapist I liked about a one-day workshop by a man named Dick Schwartz, the creator of the Internal Family Systems (IFS) model. I had heard about this model before from other therapists but never looked into it. For some inexplicable reason, this time I thought, *Why not?* and registered to attend the event the following week.

I found a spot in the auditorium as the lecture began, and I quickly found myself engaged with the material. Dick Schwartz got right into the model, explaining how he had developed it based on his work as a family therapist, one often frustrated by the limitations of the various frameworks he used to support his clients. Over time, he paid attention to how his clients naturally spoke in sessions: "A part of me hates when you—" and "A part of me loves when you—" This *parts* language intrigued him, and as he listened more carefully in his sessions, he realized these parts had distinct beliefs and roles and ways of interacting with other parts of an individual person.

I immediately resonated with this, thought about the part of me that had such empathy and tenderness for Paul and the part of me that held him responsible for my misery. Could it be they were separate parts that were polarized against each other, like the model described? I was fascinated. Not only had Dick created a map that could support therapists and clients in understanding the various relationships of the parts, but he had also uncovered that the healing mechanism to bring these parts into harmony with each other was the client's own Self energy.

He described Self energy as consciousness that can be identified by eight qualities, all conveniently beginning with the letter C: Curiosity, Calm, Compassion, Clarity, Courage, Creativity, Confidence, and Connectedness. Dick further explained that individuals are usually operating from parts of themselves that hold opinions, beliefs, roles, or agendas, and not from Self energy. For example, when someone is angry, from an IFS perspective, it can be helpful to understand that the person, the Self, is blended with a part of their personality that holds anger, and that part may be operating from a belief system it took in during a childhood event that it is now projecting on the current event. The therapist's role, he explained, is to aid the client in accessing more Self energy by unblending from the parts. It is in this state, he said, that clients connect with and witness the other parts and the roles and energy they can ultimately manifest.

He went on to explain the unblending process, and even though that step felt a little trickier to understand, I felt a warmth in my hands and a knowing in my heart: This was it. This was what I'd been experiencing within myself. I didn't know it had a name. Throughout Dick's lecture the audience had many questions and showed skepticism. I was dumbfounded at why these other therapists were having such a hard time grasping the paradigm and why they seemed to be arguing with Dick. I resolved to get trained in this model for myself and for my clients.

A year had passed since I had received that green postcard from God, and the message had been accurate. I had enough money to pay for an expensive IFS course, the children and I were living in our own house that felt like a home, I was maintaining solid friendships with Bianca and Mark, I moved through the world in a strong and healthy body, and my private practice was thriving. I was in a state of contentment. Paul seemed to have backed off, and I was sure he had because of his new girlfriend, Marie, who Jesse and Abe had been talking about. One day, while giving the boys a bath, I asked them more about her.

"Oh, that's Daddy' girlfriend," Jesse said happily.

"What does girlfriend mean to you?" I asked the boys.

"Girlfriend means they might get married and then she would be our new mommy," said Abe, splashing noisily. He was almost four, and I couldn't believe how big he was getting.

"Not our new mommy," Jesse explained to Abe. "Another mommy." He was almost seven and was often correcting his brother.

I smiled at them and said, "That's right, you lucky boys. If Daddy and Marie choose to get married, you would have another woman who loves you and cares for you. Do you like Marie?"

"Yeah, she's great, lots of fun," said Jesse. Abe nodded. "That's wonderful, boys," I said as I washed their backs. I checked in with my body. I was peaceful and happy, glad that Paul was moving on and the boys liked her. I also hoped we could move on, that Paul was done focusing on me and would enjoy his life.

Girlfriend

"You're crazy," my friend Melissa said to me when I shared the news with her about Marie.

"What do you mean?" I asked.

"Aren't you going to insist on meeting her before she becomes a bigger part of the kids' life? I mean, she's parenting your kids," she said, exasperated that she had to teach me this.

"What are you talking about?" I said, surprised. "She's not parenting my kids. Paul and I are parenting the kids. She's just hanging out with them," I said.

"Yeah, maybe for now, but if it gets more serious, she will play a big role in their life. You should definitely meet her."

This made no sense to me. I had heard this before from other divorced moms, the sit-down coffee or chat with the new girlfriend, but I had absolutely no interest in being any closer to Paul than I needed to be.

"For what purpose really?" I asked Melissa. "It's his choice and I trust he's not dating someone who is going to hurt the kids."

"You're either a better woman or you don't care as much," she said while drinking her wine. "I would absolutely die if my kid called Matt's girlfriend his new mommy."

I shrugged my shoulders and sipped from my glass.

———

I was the happiest I'd ever been, and it showed on my face and body. Since I'd been back from Arizona three months ago, I'd been making an effort with my mother and had invited her to come over to visit the boys. I had resigned myself that I would never have a relationship with her and accepted I didn't need a mother at this age, but I wanted to allow her the gift of being a grandmother, as the boys loved their time with her. It was going pretty well, and I appreciated that I could run out to a yoga class while she was looking after them. Even though the arrangement worked well for all of us, I felt a surge of adrenaline and my body stiffened every time she breezed into the house with jumbo bags of Doritos and Oreos for the kids, even though I had repeatedly asked her to cut back on the junk food. She ignored me, showering the kids with kisses and leaving bright red lipstick marks on their shiny cheeks.

If there was a hidden camera, I would have looked like a real jerk, standing in the corner watching this sweet, bubbly grandmother lovingly doting on these two little boys. "It's because your body is still in the past when it comes to your mother," said Adam when I explained the situation to him. I was seeing him about once a month, and I found revisiting the Ryzio principles helped. "It's understandable the way you watch her, guard yourself and your children," he said, "but understandable does not mean healthy." I agreed, but I couldn't seem to let go regardless of how conscious I was of the present. My wise adult just couldn't break through my anger.

Managers, Exiles, and Firefighters

The IFS trainings began, taught by Derek Scott, the man who had organized the Dick Schwartz workshop. I was looking forward to the learning but dreaded being in a room with other therapists. They always seemed to need to hear their own voices and share their personal pain. I was trying to be optimistic as I entered the house that had been rented for the course and met the nineteen therapists with whom I would spend the next sixteen weeks. The group was informal, all of us sitting on the floor or on stools around the living room, some chatting politely with each other. Derek rang a little bell to get our attention, did a quick round of introductions, and was ready to get to work. I liked his style. He was charismatic, sarcastic, and playful, the perfect teacher for me. I could sense some of the other therapists bristle when he dropped a curse word or salty phrase, but I loved it.

Derek moved through the first half of the day quickly, outlining the "parts map." He reviewed what Dick had explained about all individuals being multiples or having parts, and that these parts organized themselves into three categories. The first group consisted of *managers*, and their job was precisely that: to *manage* and help the individual function and be a contributing member of society. Derek described these parts as the parts that think for us, analyze for us, and take us to work each day. They are the parts that hold beliefs about us being polite and showing up in a way that supports us in coexisting with others in the world.

The second category of parts he described as *exiles*. Similar to the teachings of Adam, he explained that the only protection a child has in childhood is to tolerate the environment. If the surroundings are chaotic or abusive, a part will absorb the emotions, sensations, and associated beliefs, and will then be pushed into the system and out of range of awareness so that the child can continue to function and carry on. These parts carry the burdens and traumas we've experienced in our lives and are usually young in age. He described a scenario in which a child would be shamed by a caregiver or teacher, and without a trusted adult to help the child make meaning of what was happening, that child might have a part that absorbed and made meaning of that shame as "I'm bad" or "I don't have value."

Derek explained that this belief would then be held within a part called an exile because it would need to be buried deep in the subconscious. However, it could still be triggered by other life events that left the persona and internal system vulnerable to the outside world and brought that pain up to the surface. The only way the system could protect itself from this vulnerability would be to compel the managers to ensure these exiled parts didn't get triggered. For example, if your present-day boss expressed that they were disappointed with your work, that could potentially trigger an exile holding the belief that you don't have value. Therefore, the manager parts that were "people pleasers" or "perfectionists" might be used as a strategy to ensure you didn't experience the original trauma or burden unprocessed in your psyche.

If either of these last two outcomes is the case, then the third category of parts gets called into action: the *firefighters*. They're labeled as such because a triggered exile is similar to a fire in the house: It needs to be quelled immediately, put out. Derek described firefighters as urgent, quick, and strong, with the primary goal of changing the state of the system away from the burden the exile holds. "These are extreme behaviors and reactions," he explained, "such as cutting, drug use, sex, rage, and others."

"Can you give us an example of what this all looks like?" one group member asked.

"Imagine a child that is being sexually abused and does not have a trusted adult who can remove them from this horrific situation," Derek offered. "The child will have a part that will absorb the terror and whatever beliefs are associated with that experience specific to that child, such as I'm bad, it's my fault, I'm worthless. That part and its burden will be exiled by the system." He continued, "These exiles make the intolerable tolerable. Throughout the developing child's life and into adulthood, there will be triggers in the environment, such as other sexual experiences, rejection, and humiliation, that will mirror or echo the energy or circumstances the exile is holding.

Should that exile be triggered and flood the system, a firefighter that holds cutting behavior or rage may emerge. That individual may lash out in extreme ways to protect themselves from feeling the burden of helplessness or unworthiness that the exile is holding." In IFS, he explained, the therapist's work is to guide clients in their Self energy to connect with the various parts and witness and update them that the sexual abuse is over. "It's our job to help them see that it may be safe now. In doing this, we can help them unburden the trauma; release the traumatic feelings, beliefs, and experiences the parts hold; and restore them to their original energy, such as joy, peace, love, creativity."

I was nodding, all of it making sense to me intuitively. I understood that my system, like everyone's, was working automatically, programmed as Marti and Ken had described.

Get in the Closet and Pray

Thankfully, in the afternoon, the resistant participants had no more questions, and the larger group broke into triads to practice. In these triads, one group member was assigned the role of therapist, the second a would-be client, and the third an observer. I agreed to be a client first, not wanting to go first as therapist and not having the stomach for being observer and having to give unhelpful but polite feedback, which I had learned was the only acceptable way to give feedback to therapists.

"Remember, this practice is for the person acting as therapist," Derek said. "I urge those of you in the role of client not to connect to your deepest exile and painful experience. This is not therapy for you." I nodded, not interested in sharing my life with Anne, the nervous group member who had reluctantly volunteered to act in the role as therapist first. She seemed to be trying to calm herself with breathing. *Oh great, she's going to hyperventilate*, I thought. I felt myself soften: *Cut it out, and give her a break.*

"You ready?" she asked, steadying her breathing.

"Sure thing," I said.

"Okay, do you have a target part, a place you'd like to start?" she asked.

"Honestly," I said, "I have a part that doesn't like being here, that doesn't like group work. I guess we can explore that," I said. She looked terrified.

"Okay," she squeaked, "close your eyes." As soon as I did, I immediately felt the pressure to open them. I forced my eyes to stay shut. "*Open, open, open,*" I could hear in my head. I ignored it, wanting to follow instructions.

"What do you notice inside?" she asked.

I was about to give a polite answer and play along when I stopped myself and instead reported the truth of what I was experiencing. "I can hear a voice in my head yelling at me to open my eyes."

"Then open them," I heard Derek's voice. It seemed he was walking from group to group, observing, and had stopped to be with ours. As soon as I opened my eyes, my body relaxed. Anne looked at Derek, wanting him to take over.

"Go on," he encouraged her.

"Okay," she said, "with your eyes open, what do you notice?" she asked. I noticed the thought "*This chick's going to shit her pants,*" and I had to stop myself from saying so. "I hear a voice that doesn't really want to cooperate," I reported instead.

"Okay, and how do you feel *toward* that part?" she asked, repeating the line we'd learned for assessing whether clients were sufficiently unblended from parts and were witnessing from Self energy.

"I feel curious and open toward it," I said, and I was having an embodied understanding that these thoughts I have are parts, not actually *me*. I also noticed how harsh this part of me was toward people.

"Okay, okay. Good, good. Just be with it," she stammered. I brought my attention back to *it* and thought, "*Are we seriously going to sit here all day and do this?*" I sounded like a bored teenager inside. "Yeah, it's not really interested in doing this," I told Anne.

"Okay, well, ask it to step back so we can be with another part that wants to," she said while waving her hand backward.

Boom! Anger came up fast and my fists tensed, about to clench. I was surprised it had happened so quickly. It felt as if Anne had been dismissive of my inner experience and I, or this part, was ready to cut her down to size. Thankfully, I noticed this shift and felt one of those managers come online, calming me and keeping me appropriate.

Anne appeared oblivious to what was happening inside of me, but Derek tuned in: "Natasha, what are you noticing?" he asked. There was something about the way he approached me, his steadiness, that brought tears up for me. I also observed that the tears were coming from somewhere low in my belly. I breathed deeply and got curious.

"Well," I said, "there's a part in my head saying Anne sucks and it doesn't want to talk to her. There's another part in my fists that wants to destroy her, and there's a part low in my belly that is tearful, emotional about the kindness it feels from you." Anne and the other group members were silent.

"Yes, you have three parts with you," Derek continued, unbothered by my response. "Do they know you're here, with them?" he asked. I checked in again, internally bringing my awareness to the three parts, and was surprised that I could sense they knew I was with them. "Yes," I replied.

"Good, good," he said. "Ask them who they think you are, how old they think you are?" I was able to ask through my awareness, my consciousness, almost with what I imagined telepathy was like. An image came up in my head of a fragile and scared child. My eyes filled and I closed them, allowing tears to tumble down my cheeks. My group members seemed to exhale. "They think I'm little, delicate, and scared," I whispered.

"Yes," said Derek. I could see immediately that the sarcasm, the fight, and the tenderness were all playing their parts in protecting me from what they perceived as an attack on me as a small child. "I feel compassionate toward them, I have clarity about their roles, what they're doing," I said softly.

"Let them know how old you are, that you're the *Self*, present day."

I relayed the information and initially felt the confusion from these parts as they received this update, then relief. *There's more, more*, was the sense I got from inside, and yet, *not here, not with them*. I could hear that my system wanted me to be with them, to heal, but not with a group of training therapists. I silently agreed and promised these parts I would choose a therapist we could all agree on, one that felt right. "I'm good," I said to Derek. "These parts know me."

Derek looked back to Anne. He nodded to her, encouraging her to close the session. "Is there anything else any of these parts want to say to you?" she asked.

"*Her again*," I thought, and could clearly see the sarcastic teenager within me roll her eyes. I giggled and then, out loud, affectionately said to this teenager part, "Don't be an asshole."

Derek let out a belly laugh and broke the tension that was hanging over the group. "That's wonderful," he said. "This is a good teaching example that Self does not need to be some ethereal, monotone expression. Self is uniquely expressed with the qualities of the eight Cs." I beamed: Derek got me and my system. The rest of the afternoon went well, and I was happy to end the day and get back home to a hot bath. As I checked my email before bed, there was a note from Derek and a YouTube clip. "*Great work today*," he wrote, and I clicked on the link he sent. It was a clip from the movie *Carrie*, the original, with the mother snarking at Carrie and saying, "Get back in your closet and pray." At the bottom of the email, Derek had written, "*Sometimes the way my manager wants to talk to my sarcastic part.*" I laughed and laughed; so did my parts.

I approached Carol, Derek's teaching assistant at the training, the following weekend and asked if she would be my IFS therapist. I liked her. She was smart, funny, and warm, but didn't have that syrupy, therapy-style voice I hated. Carol was a full-time nurse working on a crisis team at a downtown hospital and doing IFS with patients. I asked her what this was like, providing this type of therapy in a large institution that I assumed required more of a paint-by-numbers type of therapy.

"It goes very well with my patients. They get it," she said, "and I have a good relationship with my team and managers so they stay out of my way. I'm slowly talking more about the work, educating them in group meetings by dropping some of the lingo here and there."

"No one pushes back on you?" I asked.

"Of course, some of them have resistant parts to anything new, anything outside their box. I hold Self energy toward their parts and don't push. They're not ready." She added, "Staff members who are looking for it come to my office and ask questions, and some of them have done this training and are bringing it to their patients." I thought back to my own experience working in the hospital, and it looked different from the way Carol handled it. I could see myself huffing and puffing in meetings, ensuring everyone knew I thought they were idiots, how *self-righteous* I was, how immature my behavior had been. I was pleased to see that I wasn't beating myself up for my past behavior, just noticing a better way existed. Carol agreed to be my therapist.

Peter Pan

Six months seemed to fly by between work, IFS training, and caring for Abe and Jesse. Sooner rather than later, it was the last weekend of IFS training, and I was surprised to feel I would miss this group. Over the last sixteen weeks with this crew, we'd all unearthed parts of ourselves and witnessed each other's healing. I had been successful working with my "manager" parts in my triad groups and had come to more clarity and appreciation for myself, seeing that even my judgmental and opinionated parts operated with good intentions, wanted to be better, and wanted others to be better. I also knew they could use some guidance and nurturing from Self, to be taught another way. I was looking forward to my one-on-one work with Carol and the chance to privately explore my system.

On the last day of the training, Derek offered to do a one-hour demonstration for the group with one of us as a client and asked for a volunteer. He gave us each space to check in with our parts before we raised our hands. I could feel how fast my heart was pounding. I could also hear several parts inside me want to work with Derek, want him to guide me into my system. I had asked if he would be my therapist before I had gone to Carol, and he had declined, saying, "I would love that, but I would like us to maintain our professional boundaries, as I see us doing some work together as peers in the future. You are a natural at this, and I enjoy working with you." It was such a compliment, and I really appreciated his directness.

As much as parts of me wanted to jump in to volunteer for the demo, I also felt other parts pull me back, not wanting to expose my system to the whole group. I closed my eyes and listened. I could sense parts of me dragging a chair to the center of the room, ready to go. I acknowledged them and asked them to please soften back, let me hear from the parts that had concerns. Multiple parts shared their eagerness or reluctance, and I listened to concerns about colleagues judging me, the idea that therapists aren't supposed to have baggage. I listened to other parts that didn't care what others thought, that were busy judging the other therapists in the room. I listened to all of it, calmly, until I felt that all parts would be willing to have me volunteer, even if it wasn't their preference. "Yes," I said as I got the all-clear from within.

Derek called our attention back to the room and it was time for volunteers. We were all asked to close our eyes and those who wanted to volunteer were to pick up a number between one and ten and blindly indicate it with a show of fingers. The closest to the number he had in mind would be the volunteer. I intuitively put up four fingers. "Natasha, you picked the right number," I heard Derek say warmly, and I popped open my eyes. My body felt strong and calm as I walked to the middle of the room and sat in a dining chair about a foot from Derek, also sitting in a dining chair. The rest of the group was in a circle sitting on the floor, a piano stool, ottoman, and mismatched chairs around the living room.

"Hi," Derek smiled at me, "what part are you looking to connect to?" he asked.

"Hi," I said, my voice wavering a little, the nerves coming up. "My mother has been spending more time with my children and me, and we have a challenging relationship, always have. I can't manage to be kind to her, and I treat her badly when she comes over even when she isn't really doing anything to upset me. Just her presence seems to make me angry," I said. I could sense the people around the room nodding, but I kept my attention on Derek.

"What are you noticing now?" he asked as tears spontaneously came up, and I felt myself fighting back anger and tightness in my body.

I closed my eyes and went inside myself, saying aloud to Derek, "I don't want to be so hateful toward my mother. She had a hard life and a difficult childhood; she is in pain. I just want all of it to go away." I was trying not to cry but I was choking on the words.

"Natasha," he directed, "ask this part holding sadness if it can pull back a little bit, not to overwhelm you. If it takes you over, it will kick you out and then you can't witness it and be with it." The part seemed to be responding to Derek. The intense, pleading sadness retracted a bit, and I could feel some calm restoring. "Ask this part if it's willing to allow you to go to the anger, to get to know it." I could feel the *yes* from this part, and I recognized it as the sorrow and remorse I would feel in deep waves after my mother would leave my house and I would sit at the table and cry, upset with myself for not being more appreciative of her love toward the kids, her support of me. As soon as I acknowledged the sadness, the anger returned. I could sense it in my fists.

"I can feel this anger," I said to Derek. "It feels wild."

"Does it know you're here with it?" he asked. I checked if it was aware of me. It was and I could see it, the part. The image of it surprised me. I had been expecting a big, burly guy with a machine gun, but instead it was an eight-year-old me, boyish-looking and resembling a sort of Peter Pan. It had its hands on its hips with an impish look on its face and was standing in the corner of the kitchen, looking at my mother, almost daring her to say the wrong thing. This part looked fearless and had a gleam in its eyes. I described this to Derek, watching Peter Pan walk proudly through the kitchen. "Does this part see you, know who you are?" Derek asked. I checked in with this part who was looking right at me, smiling cockily and proudly as it eyeballed me.

"Yes, it knows I'm the Self, knows how old I am. It likes me and it's proud and happy of the role it plays for me," I reported, hearing it through my consciousness, that strange telepathy that was so clear.

"And what role is that?" asked Derek.

This part looked hurt that I even needed to ask that question. "It's my protector," I said. "It makes sure no one fucks with me, gets one over on me. It's quick, clever, and fearless."

I could clearly see it was an eight-year-old energy—there was no nuance or wisdom, and it didn't care for the intricacies of decorum in the grown-up world. It didn't care if it made people feel threatened or embarrassed; its job was to make sure people knew they couldn't mess with me. Derek encouraged me to stay with this part, heart open, and ask it why it had taken on this role. The part stepped to the side and, with almost a tenderness, gestured to a whole lineup of little girls. I gasped as I saw half a dozen little girls, sweet and innocent. I burst into tears. They were so beautiful and gentle and almost angelic. I told Derek what I was seeing and tried to breathe through the tears. I felt a rush of love for these girls. Peter Pan looked up and told me with a wide grin that it had done a great job of hiding them and making sure they were never hurt. I could feel the energy of the girls—they felt like Jesse and Abe, full of love and forgiveness. As Peter Pan watched me, it sensed my love and compassion for these little girls, my genuineness toward them, and my own confidence and capacity as the Self. Its smile waned, and it looked sad, realizing that it no longer had to hide these parts, didn't have to perform its duty. "Are you sure?" it seemed to ask me. I sent a burst of gratitude and appreciation to it and let it know it was time, time to allow those beautiful qualities of those young parts to be experienced and matured through me. I let them all see Jesse and Abe, how the boys would delight in the gentle, beautiful energy behind Peter. It smiled brightly at me and moved aside, releasing the girls into my heart, and I could feel their energy moving through me. Peter did a funny little jig and seemed to salute me as the image faded.

The room outside of me was silent as I reported all that was happening to Derek. Then I was silent inside and felt myself enveloped in a blackness. Slowly, it began to lift, up, up, and up, and I realized it was the night sky. I explained to Derek what I was seeing, but it wasn't as clear as it had been when I was with the Peter Pan part.

"Ask the figuring out part of you to please soften back, allow you to be curious and for it to unfold," Derek instructed. That was better, much clearer. The night sky had a beautiful, strong, and wise energy to it. I watched the sky continue to ascend into the blackest black, and then twinkles appeared, like stars in its night sky. Then I heard a voice, like thoughts coming through my consciousness. I repeated what I heard aloud to the room: "Each star is a part of you, a part of your sky, your individual Universe. Love it and know it, care for it as yourself." The words flowed easily. Then the sky seemed to zoom out and the message with it: "And all of you, in this room and everywhere, are a part of a bigger sky, a bigger Universe, all connected and all one. Care and love yourselves and others as you." As the image dissolved, I opened my eyes and looked around the room. People were tearful, people were journaling, all were staring.

Derek looked at me and smiled easily: "Does that feel complete for today?" he asked.

"Yes, thank you," I said. "It feels complete for today."

Jesus Loves You

"Jesus loves you," came my mother's voice. It had been one week since my IFS connection to Peter Pan, and this was the first time I was seeing my mother. I had to take a few deep breaths before I could go downstairs and face her. I had been upstairs meditating, breathing, and connecting with my parts, reminding them I was an adult and we were fine, we were safe. I had started walking down-stairs, almost excited to see her, when I heard her say to Jesse, as she fed him Skittles at ten in the morning, "Jesus loves you."

I had talked to her about this a million times. "Knock off the Jesus talk and just be normal," I had said. She would tell me she under-stood, and it wasn't meant to upset me, that she wasn't aware she was doing it. I would then monitor her like a hawk the rest of the visit, ensuring she kept the Lord out in her car and not in the kids' playroom. Things would usually go fine the rest of her time with us until she'd leave, and then on her way out the door, she would call out "Jesus loves you" and slam the door quickly behind her. I would seethe. *Not today*, I thought to myself, the image of Peter Pan stepping back clear in my mind.

"Mom," I said, "I'd really appreciate it if you didn't tell the kids that Jesus loved them. We've talked about this," I said as kindly as I could. I could feel the frustration in my body, but it was less intense than before, and I was grateful that I, and not some other part of me, was doing the leading.

"Oh, okay, honey. I just keep forgetting," she waved me off. I smiled and asked her to try to remember and then quickly went up the stairs and got in the shower, feeling the anger in my body. *What the hell?* I thought. *Aren't I cured from this already?* Apparently not. I let the hot water burn my back and cool the fire in my fists. I tried to meditate but I felt pissed off, so I stayed upstairs until I distracted myself with other things. "I'm leaving now," my mom called up the stairs as I could hear the kids in front of the TV.

"Okay, thanks, Mom," I called. "Drive safe."

"Will do, honey. Jesus loves you," she yelled and slammed the door behind her. I needed another shower.

I was telling Carol the Jesus loves you story and how I couldn't seem to shake this anger at not having my boundaries respected, not being heard. She nodded. "I'm confused," I said. "You saw what happened during the demo. I talked to Peter Pan. I was healed, resurrected. Why am I still pissed?"

Carol said gently, "I know you know this from your experience with your own clients. There are layers to this. It's important you had clarity about some of your parts, but you and your mother have a long history together. There are other parts that are exiled and need healing, other protectors. Let's get curious and see what's going on," she said. I exhaled, knowing she was right. I closed my eyes and enjoyed a few deep breaths, comfortable with Carol. She guided me into my system, connecting me to thinking parts and distracted parts. They graciously softened back, and I invited up the parts connected to the Jesus loves you scenario.

Boom! I felt a strength, an incredibly powerful part that was pushing on anything or anyone. It felt massive, solid, and I could sense the loyalty and fierceness it held. Carol expertly connected me to it using the IFS protocol: How did I feel toward the part? Did the part know who I was, the Self present day? With that connection, it softened, and instantly I felt deeply grateful to this protector, could sense the duty it had to me and my system. For the first time, I wasn't angry, frustrated, or ashamed of this emotion, this expression, this part of me. I asked this soldier what it was protecting, what it was concerned would happen if it didn't hold such extreme boundaries. Images came up of me in a crummy apartment, my mother taking me to see an old church lady who ended up locking me in a closet and forcing me to take the Lord as my savior. Other images emerged, experiences of my mother praying, various relatives writhing on the floor of a church as if they had been possessed, my mean Aunt Maria-Theresa, who would clutch her rosaries while she was treating people badly. Then another image came up of me in the car with my mother. I saw myself as a young teenager, head slumped against the window, holding my breath as my mother gripped the wheel, spelling out everything wrong with me and all the reasons

I wasn't good enough. Tears came to my eyes as I saw this young girl. I knew the story, I had lived it, but when I saw this young girl in this scene, my heart called out to her, felt such deep compassion for what was happening to her.

"Does she know that you're there? This young girl, does she know who you are?" Carol asked.

"Yes, yes, she sees me," I said. I watched as this young girl, maybe fourteen or so, showed me what it felt like to sit in the car, how trapped and at the mercy of her mother she felt, the pain and heavy burden she felt in her body from having to endure. That was it! *"I have to endure, I am trapped"* was the belief and burden she was carrying. I wept, seeing how this belief had played into my marriage, my job in hospital, and my role as a parent. I could see the why of the vicious and fast fight of my soldier, protecting this part of me who couldn't withstand much more. I kept my awareness and compassion on this young girl; she could feel me, my heart and my light. I watched her as the car stopped. Her mother turned her attention to her and was ranting, getting louder and wilder.

Then, something shifted. The girl turned to look at her mother and really saw her, how the wildness and viciousness of this attack wasn't about her but about her mother's own suffering. This realization seemed to shift the heaviness the girl felt, lift the burden from her, as compassion and love came through toward her mother. I heard her say, "Mother, I am sorry you suffer, but no longer will I receive your pain, no longer will I hold it." The mother quieted, the wild franticness still in her eyes but no longer hurled at my young self. The girl opened the door to get out of the car, paused, and turned back. She took my mother's face gently in her hands and turned her to the other side, to see her own reflection in her window. With love and grace in her heart, the girl wished my mother well on her own journey, to look at her own suffering and healing should she choose to.

I was weeping as I described the scene I was witnessing to Carol. As the girl exited, I felt her freedom, her lightness, her sovereignty. She thanked me, gave me a hug, and walked down the street to begin her life with confidence and strength. When it was over, I felt my whole system updated, felt that strong soldier protector bow in gratitude in reverence for what had just occurred. I returned to the room. What needed to happen had happened. Carol was silent as she looked back at me. "Beautiful work," she said softly.

"Thank you," I said. "Yes, it was."

———

A few weeks later my mother came over again to see the boys, Sour Patch Kids and licorice spilling out of her bag at 9 a.m. I was calm and pleased to see her, really see her. When I looked at her, I saw a tired woman trying hard to please me so I would let her be with the kids she adored. This was an old woman who carried deep pain, guilt, and grief. There was also a scared young girl inside her, baffled and terrified. I offered her coffee but she declined, saying she wanted to play with the kids. She knew I was busy and would stay out of my way, she added. For the first time I could sense the pain she felt at not having a relationship with me, and I sensed her smallness and her confusion. I checked in with my body: I felt calm, peaceful. I also felt a clarity that, although I understood my mother and could forgive the trauma she inflicted on me as a result of her own, I also possessed the wisdom to know that if her pain was not healed, she was not aware or mindful of the parts of her that could hurt. I knew

I was safe, knew that I could make choices, that I could walk away from the car.

I gave the kids a kiss and thanked my mom for being there as I headed out to yoga. I felt light on my bicycle on the way to class, genuinely grateful to have her as my children's grandmother, for the love and devotion she had for them. When I got home an hour and a half later, she immediately started packing her bag, heading for the door and telling me she hadn't fed the kids too much sugar, was being more thoughtful to bring healthier snacks.

As she walked out, she said, "Jesus loves you," and slammed the door behind her. I checked in with my body. No fight. I could feel the imprint of this history between us, my back going up a bit. But it quickly came back down—a calmness spread though my body, along with the knowing that she wasn't going to stop saying it. She couldn't. It's not that she was trying to hurt me; instead, she was unaware and didn't have a hold of herself. I found myself giggling at the scene, this lady tossing her bag over her shoulder and shouting "Jesus loves you" as she ran to her car. I checked in with the boys to see how their time was with Grandma. "Great, lots of fun," they said, beaming at me, lipstick smears all over their faces where she had planted kisses on their sweet cheeks.

"Boys, what do you think about Nana saying 'Jesus loves you' all the time?" I asked.

Jesse looked at me and said, "That's just Nana. She loves Jesus and that makes her happy."

"Yes, yes, she does love Jesus. How does it make you feel when she says that?" I asked.

"It's fine. She can love whoever she wants," he said matter of factly. I looked at Abe, who appeared bored by these questions. The boys and I had a quick chat about Nana's belief in her version of God, my belief in my version of God, and that they, too, would come to their own conclusions about God as they grew up. And from that day onward, every time Nana would leave telling us that Jesus loved us, the three of us would yell back, "He loves you, too!"

CHAPTER VII

Magic D

I received an email from Paul that he was considering calling the Children's Aid Society—our area's equivalent of Child Protective Services—if I didn't stop allowing the children to visit with my family. *Seriously?* I asked, looking up above.

I seemed to have this idea that once I moved through one challenging experience, Paul's messages would stop—that I'd learned everything I needed to know to have a perfectly happy, calm, stress-free life. I was getting better at ignoring these types of messages from Paul, until my mother drove the boys to McDonald's to get French fries and didn't put Abe in a booster seat. He was five pounds away from not needing one and she didn't have hers with her. I agreed with Paul she should have the seat at all times and said I would speak to her about it. My agreement seemed to fuel him, an admission of guilt. When he demanded I end all "unsupervised contact" between the children and my parents or he was calling the Children's Aid Society (CAS), I called Susan. "What is happening? Is he serious about this?" I asked her.

"I'm calling his bluff," she said. "Trust me. CAS has bigger fish to fry than your mother." I nodded over the phone and hung up, but something didn't feel right.

I was still working with Adam sometimes, but since my time at Ryzio and work with Carol, I had less chaos in my life, had fewer fires to put out, and not so much somatic release work was needed in our sessions. My relationship with Adam was moving into one of peers rather than client/therapist, and I spent our sessions with my notebook out, getting his take on the work I was doing with my own clients and learning more about the neuroscience of healing.

"There's more than the Western modalities and science," Adam would say, and he led me to learn more about Aboriginal healing circles, Eastern philosophy, and spiritual practices. I was fascinated by all of it and devoured the resources he suggested. "Have you ever considered a plant medicine journey?" he asked me one session. We were talking about ceremony and shamans he had worked with during his time living on a First Nations reserve, studying from the elders.

"You mean drugs?" I asked stupidly.

"Plant-based medicine journeys," he corrected.

"I don't even smoke weed," I said.

Adam began to tell me about the healing properties of psychedelics and that he worked with a gifted shaman who facilitated healing journeys out of his home. "Instead of traveling to Peru, you can go to his house in the East End of the city," he smiled. "Think about it, research it. I think another deep dive would be important for you."

I went home and thought about it, curious but frightened. I was also surprised that Adam, a regulated professional, would suggest an intervention that wasn't approved or recognized by our governing body. I spent some time mulling this over, but my mind flashed to those years of training in academia and the decade of working in the hospital—how we regurgitated and replicated the same old models that had yielded little benefit to me or others I had worked with. I decided against talking to any of my colleagues about it, knowing they'd echo that same argument about professional ethics, and I resisted researching anything further myself as Adam had suggested. I knew that if I did, parts of me would scan for danger and focus on all the terrible things that could happen. I exhaled deeply, twice as long as the inhale, as I'd learned at Ryzio. That brought in some calmness and clarity. I was more curious than I was afraid, and I trusted Adam. I messaged him and asked if he would introduce me to his shaman.

The next day I received an email from Adam e-introducing me to "Magic D." I blinked twice. *Magic D?* I read the email, which was short and simple, with Adam referring to Magic D as his "soul brother." I powered down my computer and didn't think about it again until I received a direct email from Magic D inviting me to have a phone call to learn more about the *ceremonia.* At the bottom of the email in the signature was a screenshot he'd posted of a tree with a carving that read, *"And the Universe said: Everything you need is within you. You are stronger than you know. You are the daylight. You are the night. The darkness you fight is within you. The light you seek is within you. You are not alone. I love you because you are love."*

It sounded like another postcard from God or the message from the night sky during the IFS demo. I scheduled a phone call with Magic D for the following week.

"Aloha, Natasha," came the smooth, easy voice though the phone. "I'm honored to connect with you. Any friend of Adam's is welcome at my place."

"Nice to talk to you, too," I said. "I'm pretty nervous."

He laughed. "That makes sense. One thing I want you to keep in mind is that the medicine and the ceremonia we'll create together are natural but powerful tools that your Higher Self will use to take you on a journey into the deep realms of your mind, with access to a deeper state of consciousness. It requires work and disposition, and it's entirely up to you how deep the rabbit hole goes. For now, remove from your mind any expectation that psilocybin may be the right instrument of self-discovery for you." I nodded into the phone as he spoke. "Your mind, soul, and body must be in the most optimal condition to receive the medicine, so diet and preparation will be of vital importance to minimize any possible difficulty in your journey."

I was not expecting all this information and told him I was scrambling for a pen to write it down. Magic D giggled again and said, "Slow down, sister. I will go over it as many times as you like. For now, listen with your heart," he continued. "The setting of the intent for your ceremonia is an indispensable part of the preparation as well. Why do you want to do it? What is the goal you want to achieve? What area of your psyche do you want to work on? These kinds of questions will allow your mind to focus on what really is important and navigate your journey in a more purposeful way."

After we hung up, I thought about the questions he had asked. I pulled out my journal and filled page after page and remembered Magic D's words: keep it simple and from your heart. There was no heart on this page. "What I want to be different about myself after mushrooms," was the title at the top of the page. I went down the wish list of all the ways I wanted to not be who I was. The list began with number one: don't get irritated with the kids. Number two was never be triggered by Mother, and number three was never get triggered by anyone. The list went on and on about all the ways I wanted to stop being human. Overwhelmed, I closed my eyes and breathed. Tears came up slowly and gently, and I listened into them. This feeling of love and kindness toward myself came up. That feeling was how I wanted to feel toward myself and others at the end of my journey. "I want to release what no longer serves me," I wrote on my page. This was my intention.

Psilocybin

On the day of my mushroom journey, I was terrified. I was to be at Magic D's at 11 A.M. and was told to plan to be there for approximately five to six hours. That morning, I was careful how much water I was drinking, as I'd been instructed to limit my water intake and to have no food the day of. After killing time to calm my nerves, at 10:59 A.M., I locked my bicycle across the street from Magic D's apartment and whispered, "Dear God, please don't let me die in there," then headed up the stairs. My heart was pounding. The door opened. "Hello," said Magic D. The air exhaled out of me and my fear along with it. Magic D was slightly taller than me and looked about the same age. His smile was wide, and his eyes were unimaginably kind. He had a quiet yet powerful energy, and I found myself staring. I remembered his Spanish accent from the phone and recalled that Adam had told me he was from Colombia. He was dressed in what looked like a poncho made of hemp and wore slippers from the dollar store.

My mind seemed to freeze, each thought trapped in a block of ice, and all that was communicated to me was the warmth and peace in my body. It was like that standing with Marti and Ken—times a hundred. I had never felt a human being like this before. "Hello,"

I said as he waited for me to slip off my sneakers and pad into his apartment.

It was spotlessly clean and sparsely furnished, with a futon on the floor next to some meditation pillows. "Please sit," Magic D said, motioning to a table. On it were two huge books about psychology and quantum physics. He moved them aside and sat across from me, our knees almost touching, his hands folded neatly in his lap. As when I first met James, I couldn't seem to shut up. I prattled on nervously about biking over, getting there early, having no trouble finding the place, asking if he'd been living in this apartment long. I felt like a mess listening to myself, and when I looked up and saw the loving smile on his face and the serenity in his eyes, I burst into tears, covering my face with my hands, apologizing to him from beneath my fingers.

"Everything is fine," he said gently. "I am happy you are here."

I was in good hands. I didn't know how I knew this; I knew it was true. He led me into an uncomplicated conversation about the medicine, its properties, and how it facilitates healing and exploration into the "unknown," as he called it.

"Do you have your intention," he asked, "for the journey?"

"Yes," I said, "to release what no longer serves me."

He smiled and clapped his hands once. "That is a beautiful intention, wonderful. Now let us begin our preparation."

He went over to the counter, chopped some ginger, and peeled various citrus fruits, putting it all into a blender. He poured the concoction into two small glasses, served us each one, and smiled at me. "Is this the medicine?" I asked him.

"No," he said seriously, "just some delicious juice." I giggled and drank. He was right; it was the most delicious juice.

Magic D then brought out tiny rectangular cards and placed them in front of me. "Now, ask for what qualities you will need to call upon to assist you in your journey," he said. "Take a moment and meditate on that question and then select three cards."

I closed my eyes and prayed quickly, "Dear God, I'm terrified. Please tell me what I need for today. Please be with me." I opened my eyes and chose three. Magic D flipped over the first card. *Resilience*, it read. I involuntarily rolled my eyes. I was so sick of being resilient. He flipped the next card. *Acceptance*. And then the last one, *Patience*.

Magic D looked at me and asked, "What do these cards mean to you?"

I breathed out slowly. "I think these are trick cards," I said.

He giggled. "Trick cards? Oh no, no, no. I love my cards." He held the deck to his chest.

"I mean it. Those must be trick cards. My whole life, I've been resilient and I've been fighting with myself to accept anything and everything and patience is a big struggle for me."

He looked at me with soft eyes. "Yes, resilience, acceptance, and patience," he said calmly, "very important in this life." He then gave me the cards to shuffle and said he would choose three cards for what he needed to guide me today. I got the feeling he didn't normally do this but wanted to show me they weren't in fact trick cards. He placed his cards face up as he chose each one. The first, *Spontaneity*. Next, *Creativity*. His eyes twinkled. Last, *Humor*.

I burst out laughing. "Yes, these must be trick mind-reading cards," I told him. "These are the right cards for you and me today."

I laughed along with him. Magic D then pulled out his phone and set it to record, telling me to imagine I was talking to someone I really loved. I had a hard time with this, embarrassed that I was drawing a blank. I faked it and told him I was ready, and he gave me a series of words to repeat: *breathe*, *let go*, and *I love you*. He nodded, satisfied when it was done and said we were ready to begin. He took my cup from me, washed his and mine, and set them to dry. I followed him upstairs and down a narrow hallway to the journey room.

Initially, I was disappointed by how plain it looked. It had a parquet floor, a window, and a chaise, with speakers lined up next to the head of the chaise and disc jockey equipment at its feet. On the ground right by the door were meditation pillows, and in between them sat a colorfully woven mat with candles and bowls. To the right of that, against the wall, were more bowls, incense, lighters, and ash. On the other wall was a large fabric tapestry of the forest, and on the ceiling was another tapestry, this one of psychedelic colors. I looked at Magic D blankly, not knowing what to do. He smiled and motioned for me to sit on one of the pillows on the floor. He sat across from me, gently, calmly, confidently. "We begin the ceremonia," he said. He pulled out a hand-rolled cigarette and lit it, explaining that Western cultures had destroyed the sacredness of tobacco, perverting the purity of this gift from the plant. He inhaled some smoke and then exhaled it over the center of the mat between us, waving a feather and fanning it around the room. He said a prayer in Spanish as he did this and then did the same to the bowls and other items in the area. He looked back at me. "Now, we meditate," he said. He closed his eyes and sat silently. I did the same. *What am I supposed to be meditating about?* was the first thought in my head. It softened back and I was able to observe, listening to the various parts of me that were bored, scared, worried we were doing this wrong, worried we were going to die, worried we didn't turn the oven off before we left, and on and on it went. I listened to it all, coming back to focus on my breath.

Slowly, my awareness focused on a solidness in my low belly and the words *Release what no longer serves*. I felt myself become that solidness, that voice, my voice. I was calm; I was ready. My eyes were open before Magic D's and I sat there, waiting. He opened his eyes a few minutes afterward, smiling deeply, and reaching for two dried dates, one small and one large. "The medicine is in the fruit," he said. "You will take the appropriate dose based on your weight and height, and I will take a smaller dose, to be with you," he said. I nodded, a part of me scared and a part of me ready. "Everything is welcome, Natasha. I am here for you, and you are here for you," he said with love, actual love I felt in his words. I ate the large date in four chewy bites. Magic D handed me a black eye mask with what seemed to be goggles where my eyes could be open comfortably in the darkness.

I could feel him around me when the mask was on, waiting for me to lie my head down and then adjusting a speaker by my left ear, then my right ear. "Remember to breathe and let go," he said. I settled in, doing my best to let my body relax, and soon I began to hear wind and rustling from the speakers, the sounds of nature beginning to play. Then came sounds of water dripping, streaming, the wind picking up pace, the trees blowing. I felt my body relax more and tried to keep my mind focused on my breath, though it was going a million miles an hour. I could witness all of it, the calmness and the chaos, just observing. After a while, I felt a sinking sensation, as if I was falling, being pulled deep down into darkness. I began to panic, actually panic, yet I was separate from it. There was a split second where I felt the urge to get up and run out of the room, but I was afraid to do that, too. I kept focusing on my breath. Then, suddenly, I felt peace—the fear was gone, and I had the sense I had crossed over. I didn't know where I had crossed over to, but I was no longer in Magic D's apartment. I was gone.

Silly Girl

Over the next several hours, through the music he played, Magic D guided me into darkness, into light, into splendor and deep pain. My mind was clear as I watched a myriad of scenes from my life with clarity and compassion for all involved. It felt like doing IFS, but for several hours, I was being led to see, learn, and love. Some of it was painfully difficult to watch, but I observed it from a place of love. I saw my mother destroy me, my family, and herself. I saw my father's shame and neglect destroy him and us. I watched the abuse between me and Paul. I scrolled through multiple instances when I was vulnerable, desperate for attachment, when instead of approaching myself with care, I punished myself and had men abuse or use me. I watched the pain and heartbreak of what it meant to be human among humans. I cried out in compassion and sorrow for my sister, my brother. I cried out for my sons and how I kept myself sheltered from loving them too much, too deeply. And then I had to pee. I didn't know how to go about telling Magic D that I needed to get up immediately, so I called out to him. My voice sounded strange to me.

"Yes, I'm right here," he said softly.

"I'm going to pee my pants," I said.

He helped me take off my blindfold, telling me to go slowly to the bathroom. My eyes peeked open into the brightness as I stumbled across the hall. It was such a strange contrast, the clarity and sharpness I had in the darkness of the journey versus the disoriented, cloudy, and shaky feeling I had there in the light. When I returned, Magic D asked if I needed a break. "No," I said, "I'd like to go back." He nodded and helped me settle myself, taking care to adjust the speakers at my left and right side.

"How long has it been?" I asked, blindfolded again.

"Almost four hours," he said, and the music began again slowly. In a few minutes, I was back to the visions, the clear scenes, but they had changed in theme. No longer did I see heartbreak, chaos, and abuse. I saw trees, just trees, strong and seemingly wise. Light radiated from them like love, watching over everything. I saw God in those trees, always following, always present. Then an owl, steady and powerful, swooped in and landed on a limb, staring at me. I gazed back. The music became a powerful crescendo of instruments, and I was in awe of what I was experiencing in what felt like the cells of my being. "*I love you*," came a voice in the music. "*Let go. Breathe.*" I had never heard a voice more beautiful, and I felt an intense longing to be near this Being who said it. And I realized it was my voice, the one I had recorded earlier, but it didn't sound like the me I knew. This voice belonged to a me filled with pure radiating love, and I wanted to be with her.

I was overcome with sadness when I realized the voice was gone, replaced with the sound of chimes. The music shifted again, getting dark, eerie, and cold. I watched and saw a young me, maybe ten years old, running through trees, completely oblivious to their godlikeness, head down and frantic, trying to save herself. This girl was wild with fear yet steady in strength and practicality, and was loading chore after chore, errand after errand, problem after problem on her back even when they weren't hers. She was so tiny, her undertakings ridiculous and utterly stupid, yet she didn't see a choice. She didn't look up to see the light in the trees. Then came a thunderous voice inside of me: *"Silly girl, let me do this."* The tone was neither kind nor cruel, condoning nor patronizing. It was matter of fact, authoritative.

The voice was so jarring I sat up and took the blindfold off. I looked at Magic D, who was looking right at me. I burst out laughing hysterically and had to take in big gulps of air in between fits of laughter. Magic D came over and sat on the floor next to me, watching me. His kind expression sent me into more fits of hysteria. He began to laugh with me, caught up in the contagion of my fit. I was laughing too hard to explain and couldn't even form the words, but I knew I was laughing at the sheer lunacy of how I was living my life. The absolute craziness of all I tried to do by myself, the power I thought I had, and the delusion in which I lived. As the thoughts took form into language in my head, the laughter quickly turned into weeping. Magic D changed rhythms, shifting to quiet solace. He put his head down respectfully and folded his hands in his lap so I could experience all the feelings with him next to me. I reached for his hand, and he held mine with care. I looked into his eyes and told him what I saw, how I hurt myself and caused such burdens to myself by being alone, isolated, not trusting. He nodded and held my hand as I spoke. I slowly returned to calm and lay back down. The last hour was filled with lights and colors. I was too exhausted to talk with Magic D afterward. I mentioned briefly that I had seen an owl, and he looked at me with care and said, "You come back when you're ready. We will open your heart to you, to Natasha, to self-love."

Owls

I woke in the morning to an email from Magic D about owl imagery. It read, "*The owl is emblematic of a deep connection with wisdom and intuitive knowledge. When the spirt of this animal guides you, you can see the true reality, beyond delusion and deceit. The owl also offers the inspiration and guidance necessary to deeply explore the unknown and the magic of life. When the owl shows up in your life, pay attention to the winds of change.*" At the end of the email Magic D wrote, "*I feel your heart, sister. You are a brave and courageous woman. You are a magnificent container of life force. Keep strong the quest for self-discovery and self-realization.*" I took in his words. He ended with, "*Keep pushing your boundaries, extending your consciousness, challenging yourself, breathing. Our only purpose is to free ourselves from the illusory prison we've created for ourselves, so we are fully able to actualize ourselves as we truly are and not how we think we should be. My sister, breathe.*"

After the psylocibin experience, I felt more connected to nature and the Universe around me, with a new affinity for trees. Mark and Bianca noticed a shift in me. "You're less reactive," Bianca told me. "You're more here, present," was Mark's feedback. I, too, noticed I was better able to go with the flow, no longer always needing to know what was going to happen next or to plan the unfolding of each day. It was tricky for me to tell if the change was a result of the journey or the other internal work I had been doing. Nonetheless, I had started buying books on quantum physics as Magic D had and started learning about frequencies, vibrations, and how we "attract what we are." The summer was unfolding and I was happy, mostly.

CHAPTER VIII

Meeting of the Mentor

Paul was intermittently picking fights and sending messages that didn't need to be sent, issues that didn't need this much dialogue. He wrote me about silly things, at one point chastising me for getting the kids' hair cut short for summer because it didn't honor the boys' request for longer hair. I wrote back that our children had never gotten lice because we kept their hair short, and we didn't have the type of children or lifestyle of hair combing let alone styling. We continued like this back and forth until I relented. Three months later, the boys had lice.

My returned tug-of-war with Paul seemed to coincide with another bout of restlessness. When I was mindful, I got curious about my parts but was too blended to listen. I would pull from my Ryzio work and *notice what I noticed*. But I was too angry to care about noticing and instead thought of example after example of how I was being badly treated and pulled into conflicts. I was exhausted with myself, and I decided to try a meditation Bianca had sent me. She had started exploring more spiritual realms of healing and had sent me a meditation where you are connected to your Higher Self, and you can ask any question and receive guidance. I set myself up on the floor, leaning against my bed and looking out the window into the sunshine. I pushed play on the recording, exhaled, and closed my eyes. For the next few minutes, I was guided up and up, out of my body, higher and higher into the cosmos, where a portal appeared

.d my Higher Self emerged. She was breathtakingly beautiful and looked at me with immense love and kindness. I cried, feeling warm and seen. The recording said I should ask my question and listen for the answer that would come through my consciousness. "What do I do about Paul?" I asked. This beautiful Being/Higher Self smiled gently, and I sensed the answer coming to me through thought: "*Love, love is the answer, will get you to the other side.*" I resisted and recoiled, unhappy with that obscure reply. I asked again, "What do I do about my anger toward Paul?" Again, I listened and *felt* the answer: "*Love is the only thing that's real.*" I opened my eyes and stood up. I was pissed. What a stupid answer.

Source

One day, during a session with Adam, we were talking about the concepts of Oneness, the Universe, and Life Purpose when he invited me to a small, two-day workshop for a few therapist colleagues and clients who were "evolving their spiritual gifts and talents." He explained the speaker was one of his wife's teachers and mentors from Delphi University, a metaphysical training center and school in the States. I was flattered that he considered me for this type of gathering, and we discussed blurring lines in the therapeutic relationship, agreeing that I had become more of a colleague than a client over the several months since my time at Ryzio, my IFS work with Carol, and my journey with Magic D.

Adam lived way up in Leaside, about a forty-five-minute bike ride away, and I packed extra water and granola bars as I rode my bike to his house. When I arrived, sweaty and disgusting, I realized I should have taken the bus. I stood on the front porch waving my arms around, trying to cool myself, when the door opened and Adam came out and gave me a big hug. He welcomed me inside, and I saw nine other participants sipping organic tea around a gorgeous teak and glass coffee table nestled into a plush cream rug. Adam snuggled his bare feet into the carpet. He introduced me to Caren, his wife, who was tall and slender and stunningly beautiful. She gave me a warm smile and hug, then scooted behind me to check on the butternut squash she was roasting in the oven for a group snack. Adam introduced me to the others in the room, all therapists except for two, Philip and Suze, who were clients of Caren's. It felt a little like my first day at Ryzio as I scanned the room and felt childlike next to the group. I shook my head at my sweaty t-shirt, gym shorts, and backpack.

"Hi, everyone, we're about to get started," said Adam, settling on the floor across from a single rocking chair at the front of the room. Seated in the chair was a most magnificent woman. She was elegantly dressed and probably in her sixties, although it was hard to tell her age because I felt such strength, vitality, and wisdom emanating from her. It was amazing to *feel* people like Marti, Magic D, and now this woman.

"Hello, everyone," she said, "I'm Janice Hayes." After introductions, Janice moved right into teaching: "Today, we are going to create our Inner Sanctuary—a simple process, as God knows to give me things simply. If it's not simple, I'm not interested." We all chuckled. She then went on to hand out the manuals produced by Delphi and explained that the Inner Sanctuary was a meditative process that would enable us to connect directly with Source energy, also referred to by many other names, such as God, the Divine, the Universe. Janice continued: "Our spiritual Self remains in our unconscious, always trying to get our attention, until we begin our spiritual quest and become consciously aware of it."

Confused, I looked around the room. Everyone else was nodding.

Janice continued, "You may hear in some spiritual teachings that the Ego is a scourge and humans were sent to live on Earth as a punishment, but it's my belief that human beings are the most courageous, to choose to come here and experience, to expand." She motioned with her arms, "It's easy to stay a gaseous spirit, floating on Venus, but to be here, to contend with matter, to possess a mind that is constantly flitting and flopping, and emotions that shift intensely, with other human beings coming at you, well baby, that takes courage."

I smiled at her *well baby*. Her Southern accent and playfulness made this challenging material easy to absorb. "So, you see," she said, "it is important to partner with our humanness, with the Ego, because it's the only mechanism in which our spirit can feel. Without it and our human body, there is no Spirit on Earth." I was writing furiously, even though it was all written in the manual. I wanted to be sure I had all of this on paper. I was also thinking about all the time I had been spending meditating and doing yoga, engaging in these spiritual practices but not bringing the centered, calm, and clear energy from them into my actual physical life.

Janice was speaking; I was writing. "When we begin our spiritual quest and become spiritually aware, we choose to upgrade the quality of our life. We try many times and fail, because when something happens that disturbs us, we automatically react negatively. This is the old thought structure that limits us from the greater experiences." I smiled, recognizing the parallels with Ryzio and IFS, all resources and processes I'd experienced on my quest highlighting the same teaching just in different forms, different languages, all guiding me to wholeness and peace.

Janice continued, saying, "We need to establish a new structure of thought with positive responses that attract positive experiences and feelings of self-worth and confidence. Your Inner Sanctuary is your new structure, and once it is established, our positive and loving responses become as automatic as the negative reactions were."

Janice taught for the rest of the morning about Light and Energy in ways I had never heard before. She also referenced the Law of Attraction, something I had been reading about but that my practical self couldn't get my head around. I preferred the way Janice taught it, simply saying, "Whatever you're thinking produces mental images that form an emotion. Those images and emotions carry an energy that will move through the physical barrier and will attract people, situations, and circumstances that confirm those thoughts and feelings." She said, "Think of your thoughts as an arrow." She lifted her arms like she was holding an imaginary bow, closing one eye like she was aiming it. "And think of your emotions as a bow." She acted as if she was pulling the arrow through. "The thoughts aim the arrow; the emotions propel it forward." She released her hands like she was releasing it to shoot toward a bullseye.

"If you are spiritually unaware, you will think and feel that you are a victim of the world. It appears you are, but you fail to realize you are the creator of your world through your thoughts and emotions." She placed her hands back in her lap. "Eventually, you will learn to release all feelings of unworthiness and helplessness and create each day anew." *Here's hoping*, I thought, ironically aware of that thought arrow.

After the arrows, the group took a break and I went outside for a few minutes, still too intimidated to mingle. I checked my messages and found myself feeling disappointment to not get a message from someone who loved me, checking in on my day. I wanted a partner; I wanted affection and companionship. I was beginning to want. I brushed away these feelings by looking around Adam and Caren's lovely neighborhood and the strong, solid trees strewn about it. Then I turned around and went back inside to learn how to connect to God.

Inner Sanctuary

For the remainder of the morning, Janice began to walk us through the creation of the Inner Sanctuary—a Spiritual Complex, she called it—that contained rooms we would visit in sequence. "There is order, structure, and harmony within our Inner Sanctuary that restores order, structure, and harmony in our life," said Janice. We were instructed to close our eyes and follow our breath as Janice guided us in a visual meditation to the first room, which she called the Spiritual Gym. As I did in IFS training, I followed Janice's voice as she guided the group, and I could see in my mind's eye an image of a room that was dark except for a boxing ring, illuminated with a large, white punching bag in the center. Janice instructed us to walk up to the bag and punch it, throwing our might into releasing any and all negativity we held in our bodies, in our thoughts, and in our hearts. *"No problem,"* I thought. Anger, desperation, despair, and loneliness flooded through me as I visualized my hands smashing the bag, and I saw darkness release from my fists. "Punch out that negativity and watch it be transformed to light," Janice said, "and if you have nothing to let go of, punch it out for the world, for the earth, for humanity."

After a bit, she instructed us to enter the Healing Room, where we would meet our Higher Self. Exhausted from punching, I dragged myself to this next area and, using my consciousness, opened the door. It was light and airy inside, like a spa. Janice had us bring our awareness to a second doorway where our Higher Self would enter. I held my breath. All of a sudden, I saw a woman round the corner and meet my eyes. Warmth washed through me, followed by grief and pain. She looked like the most glowing, loving, and gentle me that I could ever hope to be. I was reminded of the voice I had heard during my journey with Magic D. My Higher Self opened her arms and I fell into her and let myself be held. Softness washed through my body.

Slowly, Janice directed us back to the external reality of Adam's living room. I opened my eyes and looked around the room and felt closer to every person in there. During the break, I was chatting easily with some of the therapists, getting to know more about their practices and intrigued to hear how they integrated their spiritual knowledge and experiences with their clinical work. I saw Janice talking in the living room to a small group, answering questions about the Universe. I filled my water cup and tried to be casual, taking a seat near her, but I wanted to talk to her about my tug-of-war relationship with Paul and what she meant by attracting that experience. When there was a pause in the conversation, I asked Janice if I could speak with her privately. "Well, of course, hello," she said. I tried not to get lost in the backstory, but I couldn't help it, and the examples of the horrible dynamic between me and Paul kept tumbling out of me. "Are you trying to change him, control him?" she interrupted me, a serious expression on her face, her gaze steady as her eyes affixed themselves to mine.

"Well, I'm trying to get him to stop being a maniac," I said, an attempt to be funny and charming that instead left me feeling silly and ashamed.

"Well, if your thoughts are focused on what to tell him or how to *help* him be, how you would like him to be, I would look at that," she said. I stared at her blankly, confused. "It's okay, baby cakes," she said, her Southern accent even stronger. "You haven't known a greater way than what you've been doing. The personality has been habitually repeating this process again and again with the same negative result. You are here today to expand your awareness with a greater way of consistently *going within*," she said. I looked at her calmly, though I was still confused as to what I was supposed to do in the physical with Paul. "Ask yourself," Janice continued, "are you working to be right or make it right? Because any time you insist on being right, it usually means somebody else is wrong. This causes separation. The path is to make it work. Those with spiritual *maturity* bite their tongue often. They give people freedom to believe what they want." I stared, looking at her blankly, thinking maybe it was that Janice wasn't getting the full extent of what this divorce had been like. Either way, I thanked her and stepped outside to think about what she had said.

For the rest of the afternoon, we worked our way through some of the other rooms of the Inner Sanctuary, each beautiful and filled with lessons. By the end of the day, I was spent and did not want to get back on my bike. I gladly accepted a ride from Philip, leaving my bike behind. On the drive home, we got to know each other, and I felt I had been close to him my whole life even though we had merely exchanged pleasantries throughout the day. He said he had been divorced for a few years, and it had been an ugly mess. When his marriage "blew up," he said, he started working with Caren. "I've done some amazing work with her," he said. "Caren seems to think I have some talents and gifts, and she has been a real mentor to me. Adam must feel that way about you or you wouldn't be here."

"I guess," I said. "I just want to have peace; I want to stop fighting everyone. I want to be free."

"Yeah," said Philip, "peace and freedom. Two days ought to do it," and we both laughed.

Victims, Talkers, and Initiates

"There are three types of people," Janice was saying at the beginning of our second and last day of the workshop. "The first type are *Victims*, who find themselves involved in negative circumstances continually. They are unaware of their inner resources, spiritual strengths, and abilities. They consistently blame others, circumstances, and events for their problems. They are vulnerable and have no control of their thoughts, emotions, and behaviors." I couldn't write fast enough, abandoning my coffee and scribbling.

"The second type are *Talkers but not Walkers*. This group is mentally aware of Spirit and can express wisdom to others, but cannot apply it in their personal life." I nodded, images of some spiritual leaders and gurus I'd been reading about coming to mind.

"*Spiritual Initiates* are the third type, and they are spiritually aware and committed to manifesting goodness and plenty. They take the responsibility for positive solutions and respond with wisdom and love. They accomplish this through desire, spiritual knowledge, and their own spiritual, mental, and emotional development." I stopped writing and categorizing others and wondered what type I was. I knew I had spent much of my life in the Victim category and wondered how much time I was spending in the second. I sat up a little taller; I was so wanting to be an Initiate.

"You cannot control the situation you find yourself in," Janice continued, "but you can alter your old structures of negative reactions and shift to more positive responses." She looked around the room and we all nodded. "When you find yourself in this negative reaction, go to your Inner Sanctuary, work thorough the various rooms toward the Insight Chamber. Here, you will ask your question and receive divine guidance and inspired wisdom as to how to proceed in any situation."

My body was tingling everywhere. I had so many questions and was hungry for more guidance and support when it came to my future, past, and present with Paul. Janice spent the rest of the morning guiding us through the rest of the rooms in the Inner Sanctuary, leading us to the Insight Chamber. After the Spiritual Gym and Healing Room, we entered our Restore Room; our Mountain Room, where I climbed rugged peaks to achieve my goals; and our Dolphin Room, where I learned to play.

It was time for another break, everyone filing into the kitchen for tea and snacks. When I took my phone off airplane mode, my heart sank. It was a buzzing message from Paul, in all caps, demanding to know where I was. The school had called. *Fuck.* I was simultaneously terrified about re-engaging in a tug-of-war with Paul and that something horrible had happened to one of the boys. I walked away from the group and checked my voicemail. "Hi, Natasha, it's Julie calling from the school. Everything is fine, but Jesse says he's not feeling well, so I'm calling to see if you want to pick him up, thank you," she said cheerfully. I checked the rest of my text messages, several of them from Paul, one after the other accusing me of abandoning the boys when I was at my workshop. All I could think about was the child services and that this confirmed that I was a selfish, unfit mother. I saw another message come in, this one from my friend Wendy: "Dude, you okay? Paul called me looking for you. Said you'd gone missing." Paul had sent an email to my lawyer, Susan, with me cc'd, saying I had gone missing. Every single text message, email, and phone call, including the initial call from the school, was from the forty-five minutes that I was trying to connect to God.

Janice was holding a cup of tea, blowing on it as she walked into the living room. "I have to leave," I blurted. "My kid is sick—I mean, the school called and his dad has lost it and he wrote my lawyer and I just need to—"

Janice interrupted. "Is anybody hurt?" she asked.

"No," I said, "but Paul will lose it. He'll—"

Again, Janice cut me off: "Stop."

"You don't understand," I argued. "He's made my life hell and—"

Snap! What seemed like the loudest sound I had ever heard came from Janice's fingers. It worked. She had popped me out of my panic.

She looked at me sternly. "Go upstairs and punch," she said, pointing toward the stairwell.

"But I have to respond. I have to," I started.

"You just said that no one is hurt, correct?"

I nodded.

"The only thing happening is you getting caught in this energy, this dynamic with him. Go upstairs and punch in your gym."

I could feel the parts of me screaming I had better leave. But in the face of the solidness of her, I trusted.

Punching

I sat on the cold, tiled floor of Caren and Adam's bathroom, my back against the closed door, to envision my Spiritual Gym. Eyes shut tightly, I could see the punching bag, the dark room with the ring illuminated in the center. I punched. I punched with my mind, and I physically punched with my fists. The thoughts started separating enough that I could hear them: *You're going to get in trouble.* Punch. *Get home!* Punch, punch. *You've lost your mind, you've truly lost your mind!* Punch, punch, punch.

I kept going. Then, *Fuck him, fuck him, fuck him.* Punch, punch, punch. *Everyone just stop, leave me alone!* Punch, punch. *I want to be free! I want to be safe.* Punch, punch, punch. I punched out all the shame I felt at failing Abe and Jesse as a mother. I punched out all my rage at Paul, all the blame and control in our relationship. I punched and I punched and I punched. More light and more light and more radiant light poured into that gym and all around me. Then, silence.

It was quiet. I was empty; it was done. It was a very strange experience for me to not feel strong emotions. I stood up, calm. I saw I had missed some phone calls. I turned off my phone and walked out of the bathroom, slipping the phone into my backpack, and went back to the group. Janice nodded at me and continued talking, not missing a beat. She was saying, "Each person is responsible for their own quality of behavior, and we are responsible for our own." The worried parts nagged at me in the background. I didn't ignore them; I just didn't blend with them. I felt a solidness in my low belly and cleared my head and followed along with the group as we approached our Insight Chamber.

Insight Chamber

In the Insight Chamber, I would meet again with my Higher Self. I could ask any question and be given divine guidance. With my eyes closed and under Janice's direction, I pushed open heavy, wooden double doors and walked into a most wonderous room, its walls lined floor to ceiling with books. In my mind's eye, I settled in a comfortable leather chair. My Higher Self entered, every bit as radiant and peaceful as she had been in the Healing Room. I asked her, "*What do I do right now in this situation with Paul?*" She smiled with her eyes, with her whole being, and I heard, "*Do nothing. Be still.*" I opened my eyes to Adam's living room and jotted it down in my notebook. *Be Still.*

Next came the Creative Laboratory. Janice explained that we, as human beings, are shaping light with our intentions all the time. In this Creative Laboratory, we would shape the light to manifest the guidance we received in the Insight Chamber. Janice went on to comment that in this Laboratory, you create your heart's desires. She winked. "If you want a red Ferrari, create a red Ferrari," and everyone in the room laughed. "Always think of what you are man-ifesting in the present tense, as though it exists. Imagine yourself enjoying your vision with as many details and dimensions as you can," she said.

I closed my eyes and saw a big, white door with light streaming out of the top and bottom. I walked in and created. I created myself sovereign, free, still. I created a life of joy and ease. I saw myself with Jesse and Abe, laughing and loving them. I saw myself in a larger home, a bedroom for each boy. I saw myself taking long baths and reading. I saw myself in the arms of a man who made me feel protected, loved. I saw myself at peace.

Janice directed us out of our Laboratory, trusting our creations were on their way to us, and into the final room: the Sacred Room. I felt God in this space. It was light, filled with tall, strong trees that were loving, gazing down on me, watching over me in my life, a reminder always to be still and let the world and Universe move around me, drawing love toward me and shielding me from harm. Among the gentle streams and ponds; clean, magnificent air; and rich, deep soil, I was part of all of it. I felt Oneness. I opened my eyes and looked around the room. It was the same room, but I felt different in it, saw it differently. I felt peace. I looked over at Philip, wondering when he'd be getting a Ferrari.

At the end of the day, I gathered my things, ready to reflect on Janice's words to me. I had stood up, feeling strong and confident, and heard parts of me that were warily trusting me, still holding firm to the logical belief I should have at least told Paul I was alive, I had gotten his messages, and I hadn't been kidnapped or hit by a car. These parts knew that was the responsible thing to do, the courteous thing to do.

I asked Janice about this as everyone was filing out of the room. She looked at me as I approached and said, "You get trapped in that energy, you and Paul, dancing this dance over and over again."

"Can you help me understand that?" I asked, "Shouldn't I respond if there's an emergency, or just out of courtesy?"

"Was there an emergency?"

I hung my head. I had spent the day with God inside myself and this incredible teacher, yet I could easily be confused and sit in doubt. "When this energy with Paul comes toward you, you have a choice. Engage it or let it go by," she said, moving her hand back and forth in a swimming motion. "If you won't play with it, it will find someone that will. These are tests and challenges in your life—everyone has them during their lifetime. They are your opportunity to demonstrate your mastery. How do you know if you've mastered something if you don't test it? Remember that it's easy to love the loving. It is much harder to bring love and understanding to someone who is not so loving."

"Thanks, Janice," I said, giving her a huge hug.

"Go to your Inner Sanctuary every day for thirty days and ask, ask for your next step," she said.

"Today it told me to do nothing, to be still," I reported.

She laughed. "Yes, I have been told that many a time. So very wise," she grinned. "And," she continued, "every day, sit in your meditation and send Paul love and light. Every day, sit there until you can do that. If you do this, watch what happens at the end of thirty days."

I hugged her. "I love you," I said.

"I love you," she said, and I knew she meant it. So did I.

I had been riding home for about fifteen minutes when I pulled over by Mt. Pleasant Cemetery, leaned my bike and myself against the gate, and pulled out my phone. There were several messages from Paul, the last telling me he was keeping the children overnight, as I was clearly an incompetent parent. I checked in with my body, checked in with my parts. It was eerily quiet; I felt like a tree. Still and strong, I replied to Paul, "Hi, I'm glad the boys are okay and thank you for picking them up. I was in a course all day with my phone off. I'm happy to pick up the boys from you or will make the time back as you suggested. Let me know what you choose."

I looked at the message and checked in about my intention, the energy the message carried, and outcome I visualized. *Peace* was the answer to these questions. I pressed send and made my way home.

CHAPTER IX

Tests and Challenges

It had been a week since the Inner Sanctuary, and I was getting daily messages from Paul about time I owed him, how irresponsible I was, how he had missed an important work meeting, how much the boys had suffered. Each time, I would get pulled in, feeling myself get more rageful, terrified, and guilt ridden. Then I would curse Janice, curse God, and curse personal growth, which seemed to be doing nothing but shrinking me. I followed the guidance of my Inner Sanctuary to *Be Still*, and I did not respond. And each time, after I didn't respond, I would curse everyone, sit on the floor, close my eyes, and punch in the Spiritual Gym. There was always a skeptical part of me that believed I was delusional to be exploring inner landscapes as my external life was falling apart, but I reasoned that doing this work was better than doing crystal meth. After some soothing and support from my Higher Self, I would make my way through the rest of the rooms in the Inner Sanctuary, getting to the Insight Chamber, where I would ask from my heart my next step. For a solid week, it was the same: *Be Still*. I'd like to say I accepted this message with grace, but I didn't. I yelled back inside my head and outside into the room, *"I can't be still when there are real life threats and consequences!"* Yet the message was unwavering: *Be Still*. So, I did nothing with Paul's messages, letting them come one after the other.

Root Like a Tree

One day, while coming out of the Inner Sanctuary, I looked at the OurFamilyWizard app and scanned the messages. I realized that not one message contained a matter that needed my attention or communication around the kids' needs. We had two separate households with separate belongings for the children, and the pick-up and drop-off were done at the school. The separation agreement and parenting plan were rock solid and comprehensive. There was absolutely nothing that warranted this much contact from Paul: it was all about anger, bitterness, and resentment. I reflected on that day that Janice snapped her fingers at me.

Janice's teachings came to me—how we shape the light, our reality, and life circumstances based on our intentions, perceptions, and choices. I had no control over Paul, only myself and how I responded. I would *be still* until I could create from a different energy, different intention. In that moment, I began to send Paul love and light, realizing I could only do it after I punched out all the anger and hatred, after receiving soothing and support from my Higher Self and wisdom and guidance from the Insight Chamber. Once that was complete, I could go to my inner Creative Laboratory and create the healthier dynamic I wanted to experience. I knew not to change Paul, so I left him out of it. Instead, I created myself as a tree: solid, wise, and rooted. I was strong and reasonable, my branches and limbs able to sway and bend but never to bend so far that they would break the legal agreements and contracts rooting us both. Afterward, I would say a prayer, imagining Paul and enveloping him in light. I would tell him I loved him, I would tell him to let me go, and I wished him well.

After four days of this practice, I got an email from Susan letting me know that Paul intended to call the Children's Aid Society (CAS). Rage coursed through me. It was so powerful it frightened me, like I could flip a car or level a building. I needed to move my body because there was no way I could sit with this much adrenaline, even to punch in the Spiritual Gym. I threw on my sneakers and went for a jog; actually, it was more like rage running in the street. When I was exhausted, I dragged myself back home to reread the email from Susan. It was an FYI that she had received an email from Paul's lawyer with an attached journal entry, one I had written years before. I opened the attachment and felt my body sink, my mind beginning to race. I read the forwarded message from Paul's lawyer:

Susan,

> *I had a phone call with my client, and he says he is not trying to harass Natasha in any way, but he is however very concerned about the children being alone in the care of Natasha's parents. For context, I am sending you an email that he has sent me, which Natasha wrote and forwarded to Paul so that he would have a copy. You will see this email makes very serious allegations against her parents and repeatedly says they are not safe and she will not allow her children to be exposed to them. If there have been dramatic changes, Paul is happy to hear about them and that can be discussed at another mediation appointment. All that we need for now is a confirmation the children are not going to be left alone with Natasha's parents pending further agreement or direction from a mediator. If*

Paul doesn't get that confirmation, he says his next step will be indeed to contact Children's Aid Society.

I look forward to hearing from you.

Best, Kevin

I looked at Susan's response to Paul's lawyer:

There will be no such agreement. He can call the Children's Aid.

S

"I'm calling his bluff," Susan said when I phoned her.

"I know that," I said, "but did you read the attachment?"

"I skimmed it," she said evenly. I could feel her embarrassment for me, having my personal writing emailed to lawyers.

"It wasn't an email to Paul," I explained. "It was a diary entry that I forwarded to him, sharing myself."

"Out of context, it's dangerous," Susan said flatly. "He's leveraging this to continue to engage you. It's up to you how much you want to keep putting up with."

Children's Aid

Later that week, I was checking my voice messages after a good day of client work and heard, "Hello, Natasha, my name is John, and I work for the Children's Aid. Our agency has received a safety concern about Jesse and Abe. Please call me back at this number." I looked out my office window and saw the tall trees. "Where are you?" I whispered. "Please be with me." There was only silence, stillness.

I called the number and John explained that, based on a concern and complaint made by Paul, there was now an active file, and he would have to come out to interview the children. I told the kids that a social worker, like Mommy, was coming to visit the house and ask them some questions. "This happens sometimes," I told them. "When parents have different houses, sometimes workers come to visit because they know two houses can be a big step for families. He'll ask you two a few questions. He's here to help." Jesse nodded, seemingly satisfied. Abe went back to making a mess of his breakfast.

On the day of the visit the house was clean and so was I, dressed in professional clothes, my hair brushed. I picked up the kids at school a little early, gave them a fun snack, and reminded them that a social worker named John was coming. I didn't feel nervous about the visit, but I was plenty nervous about Paul, the lengths he'd go to. I had checked in with my Inner Sanctuary earlier that morning, hearing from the Insight Chamber, *"Be still, be peace."* Within an hour, I was paranoid and furious. This spiritual path of trusting and allowing was not for the wimpy, Janice had said. "There aren't any tulips on this road. First, the storm, then the rainbows." I knew this was my storm, but it wasn't on the outside, wasn't happening to me. It was on the inside.

Throughout my meditations and reflections, I could see my ups and downs, my triggers, my emotions somersaulting at any given moment. I had this internal storm, this internal chaos. I was proud of myself for working toward consciousness, and I knew Janice was right. I understood the phrase *As above, so below* and that like attracted like. I was committed to shifting my internal world to more peace, to attract it in my external life. I was communicating with my parts every morning in the shower, where I did my best healing, when they could soften back enough to connect to me. This was effort, working with myself to respond to my environment in new and conscious ways, to update my programming.

Jesse and Abe raced to answer the door, loving the act of welcoming people into our home. "Hello! Would you like a tour?" they said in unison. John smiled and said hello, joining me in the kitchen. He shook my hand, gave me his card, and accepted the glass of water I offered. The four of us sat at the table.

"So, did your mommy explain to you who I am and what I'm doing here?"

Jesse nodded and said, "You help families, and you're here to see what we need help with."

John smiled. "Yes, that's right. I'd like to ask you boys some questions about what it's like being at Mommy's house and Daddy's house." The boys nodded, apparently comfortable with John. "Maybe we could start with your offer of a tour," he said to the boys. They scrambled up from the table, excited to start with their room and work their way up. It would have been really funny to hear Jesse point to the lighting and say, "And Mommy loves pot lights, so we have lots of them," if he weren't reporting my interior design preferences to a child protection worker. John giggled.

Back at the kitchen table, John asked if I would excuse them, that he would like to talk to the boys individually and together. I looked at four-year-old Abe and seven-year-old Jesse and felt a pain in my heart. It wasn't panic, fear, or protectiveness; it was sorrow for them and this experience. I looked at the kids steadily, calmly, and asked, "Is that okay with you boys?" They smiled eagerly, enjoying this attention from John. "Okay," I said. Abe went upstairs with me to play so John and Jesse could talk. I could faintly hear them, and Jesse was talking a lot, laughing at times. John then invited Abe down, and Jesse came up to read and play. "He's a nice man," said Jesse, hugging me and then scampering off to find his favorite book.

Ten minutes later, John invited us to gather again at the table. "These are very clever and wonderful children you have," he said.

"They are pretty fantastic," I agreed, and the boys beamed.

"I asked them to draw me some pictures, showing me what they liked about Mom's house and what they liked about Dad's house," he said, pointing to the sets of drawings. It appeared that they liked video games and play time at Daddy's house and story time and play at my house. Made sense. "Then I asked them about what they liked doing with Nana. They said that Nana played fun games with them, brought them lots of treats, and was lots of fun." I nodded. "Then I asked them to draw for me what they didn't like about Daddy's house and your house," he said, and I watched as he spread out pictures. "Both boys said they didn't like when you and Daddy got angry." I nodded because that also made sense. John continued, "And I talked to the boys about how mommies and daddies have lots of feelings, some that feel good and some that don't, and the boys said they can talk to you both about their feelings, which I said was a very good thing for families." I smiled at Jesse and Abe. "About their Nana," John said, "both boys said they don't like all the kisses with her lipstick stuck on their faces."

"She does give lots of lipstick kisses," I agreed. "We will have to talk to her about that if it doesn't feel good." Both boys looked so pleased, hearing their needs coming from a third party. My sorrow had softened. I felt still.

John got up to leave and shook both boys' hands, asking them if it was okay if he talked to me alone. The boys ran off for some TV time. John turned to me. "You have lovely children. You have done a good job," he said sincerely. "Thank you," I said. He started to pack up his things, saying, "I don't have any concerns. But I am not yet able to close your file until I speak to your ex-husband about my observations."

"Thank you," I said again.

When John left, I headed upstairs and wedged myself between the two boys to watch *Transformers* with them. We were going to have ice cream for dinner.

CHAPTER X

Road Back

I was sitting against the bed, struggling with sending Paul love and light, especially with so much anger and resentment about him calling child protection. *It didn't have to be this way*, I thought, moving through my Inner Sanctuary and approaching the Insight Chamber when it came to me: why Paul couldn't let me go. It was because I didn't let him go.

In our tug-of-war, I was still holding my side of the rope. I sat in stillness and observed what was playing through my consciousness, a vision of Paul and the divorce from his perspective. I saw how afraid he had been of me putting my energy on my career, how threatening that was for him, and his parts holding burdens from his own childhood. I saw how he perceived me as abandoning him and the boys, rejecting my life with them, how he experienced me moving on quickly as an indication that I was unfeeling and selfish.

I also saw his anger at having to then pay me thousands of dollars in child support, having to sell our beautiful family cottage while knowing I wanted nothing to do with him. I could see how it had happened so fast for him, yet so painfully slowly for me because of my feelings of being trapped. The images began to shift from Paul as angry and attacking to the boy inside the man, frightened and abandoned. I felt compassion for him and at the same time love for myself, not wanting to put myself in a position where my empathy took over and I felt responsible for his feelings or behaviors. I had been learning about the distinction between empathy and compassion, how they can feel the same at the beginning, but they lead to different outcomes. Compassion runs along the neural pathway associated with pleasure—feeling care toward someone and the pain they are experiencing. Empathy runs along the pathway associated with pain—feeling care for someone and experiencing their pain with them. I closed the meditation, sending Paul love and light and telling him to move on. I was dropping my side of the rope.

Divine Love

Things were quiet at home with the kids, and I hadn't heard anything from the Children's Aid Society in over a month. My experiences in meditation and the Inner Sanctuary were lighter, more peaceful, and I was spending less time in the Spiritual Gym and more time in the Creative Laboratory, manifesting a new house for myself and the boys. I was proud of my current little townhouse, setting up this home, but I had always felt a tug as I watched the boys head down to the basement to sleep in their bunk beds in a small room below-ground. I knew we were fortunate, privileged in fact, cognizant that my father had slept with his two brothers wedged on either side of him on barely a mattress while his four sisters were sharing another flimsy bed. But I also thought about what Janice had said about visualizing a Ferrari if you wanted a Ferrari.

There didn't seem to be any guilt or shame in asking God for things from a place of love and appreciation, not greed. I realized my guilt and shame was a human thing, a culture thing, not a God thing. So, with gratitude in my heart, I went to my Creative Laboratory every day and visualized myself walking around my new house with its three big bedrooms, gleaming hardwood floors, and brilliant stained-glass windows. When I was done visualizing myself in my new house, I moved on to creating a relationship anchored in *reliability, predictability,* and *consistency.* When it came to intimate relationships, Janice had talked about love during the training; I had been so spun out about Paul, I hadn't absorbed all of it.

I was grateful for my furious note-taking and took time reflecting on her teachings about differentiating between Divine Love and Human Love, which she explained as *attachment love.* Janice said that the love between children and their parents is attachment based—*I love you so you will help me survive.* She then described teenage love as hormonal love, the beginning forms of love needed to perpetuate the human race, as most forms of human love are a form in which to attain a need. This was the same with Romantic Love, which was premised on *I need you to love me back,* which was based on control and the unconscious fear of being alone. Janice taught that the closest human love gets to the truest expression of love is *caring.*

Divine Love, on the other hand, is impersonal and not an emotion but a state of being. "The sun shines on the just and unjust. It's for everyone," she quoted. She likened Divine Love to a heart beating, pumping blood equally to all the organs, not judging between the ones that digest our food and the ones that manage the elimination of waste. The heart sends a constant flow of nourishment and support, and it never wavers. After reading Janice's wise words, I decided to do a meditation and go into the Insight Chamber to ask about relationships. I had begun to feel a wanting, a wanting for partnership. "*Do nothing, just Be,*" came the response through my consciousness. I hated that answer. I asked again. "*Just Be,*" came the response.

EMDR

Several of the IFS therapists I had met in my training with Derek had talked about Eye Movement Desensitization and Reprocessing (EMDR). I had started looking into it, curious, but it didn't resonate with me the way IFS had. In fact, when I first saw a therapist on YouTube sitting in front of a client and waving his fingers back and forth in front of their eyes to stimulate the client's processing of past trauma memories, I thought it was ridiculous. I had heard of this years ago while working at the hospital and dismissed it outright, as the rest of my clinical team had. But as I knew more about what was possible in the realm of healing, I was eager to see if I could bring this modality to my clients and maybe benefit from it myself. Even though I was doing well, meditating daily, checking in with parts and living more from a place of my wise adult, I still found myself spending more time in the shower than I'd wanted, my only sure-fire strategy to keep myself from reacting from my old program. I was grateful to be operating less from that place, with the intensity, duration, and frequency of strong emotions decreasing for me. In this way, I knew *the work was working*, but I also knew there was more. I signed up for the intensive weeklong EMDR training and was delighted to hear—despite my initial irritation with her—that Anne, my fellow IFS therapist-in-training, would be doing it, too.

———

Anne and I had come a long way together since our adventure in training. This time, I was grateful she was in this intensive, weeklong training. We were especially glad to be together because the large group was required to break up into pairs to practice what we were learning. Over lunch the first day, she and I contrasted IFS with EMDR. Both were targeting past trauma, but whereas IFS worked with trauma trapped in exiled parts, EMDR targeted trauma stored in memories embedded in neural pathways in the brain. After the first day, I had the general premise and understood that when the trauma memory is triggered in present day, it activates the sensations, beliefs, and emotions stored along with the actual event, almost as if all of it had been frozen in a block of ice. It was similar to how Adam had first introduced me to the concept of dual attention: clients are aware this is a trauma memory from the past that they are going to witness, not relive. Once that concept is established, eye movements are introduced, or some other type of bilateral simulation, like tapping alternate shoulders or knees.

Especially cool to me was how the technique was discovered. In the 1980s, Dr. Francine Shapiro had noticed her patients looking off to the side or up and down when they were recalling their childhoods and past traumas. She realized that the occipital lobes and other regions of the brain were connected to various parts of the memory system. She also realized that REM sleep is the eyes moving back and forth to update the more emotional and intuitive information—held in the right brain—to the left brain, which holds logical, rational information, and is responsible for orienting us in time and space. It appeared that trauma in the developing childhood brain interrupted the pathway from left to right brain; therefore, the information never got updated. By stimulating this cross-brain connection, the brain's own innate wisdom and intelligence would organically update the brain and the traumatic beliefs, sensations, and emotions to a healthier and more adaptive understanding of the past event. I was excited that it overlapped with the internal healing I had been exploring elsewhere, like at Ryzio, with IFS, and in the work with Janice.

On day two of the training, I realized that EMDR wasn't just a technique but a therapeutic model rooted in a trauma framework.

We learned that there were eight phases, which captured the model's focus on establishing safety and stability in the client's system. We then moved to the processing of traumatic memories, and then to reintegration and reconnection. Throughout the week, Anne and I paired off and played therapist to each other, working on simple erroneous beliefs and experiences rather than trauma memories—nothing that would be too intense in a training setting. I knew I needed an experienced therapist to work with me and felt drawn to Oriana, one of the training staff, who seemed able to integrate IFS parts work with the practice of EMDR.

Trust

Oriana was in her late forties, married, and had four children, along with a thriving teaching and private practice. She was brilliant, confident, and humble. I loved her immediately. At that appointment, we were going to begin processing. "I can't trust anyone," I said. "I look at my life and I'm alone. I do everything on my own and I'm tired. And I know EMDR is about processing memories, but I can't seem to isolate a specific one. There are so many different things it could be."

Oriana nodded, comfortably sitting in her chair while sipping a cappuccino she'd just made while I was entering her office. "Okay, let's stay with the feeling that's coming up, the belief that you can't trust anyone. We'll find our way to the memory," she said. She moved to a spot across from me and off to the right, our knees parallel to each other, and sitting far enough away from me that her outstretched arm could wave back and forth across my line of vision. She asked me to go inside myself, connect with the part holding the belief

I can't trust anyone. I closed my eyes and saw my dad, feeling a wave of intense anger and sadness.

Oriana and I established the intensity of the somatic experience, and I was instructed to breathe and allow whatever images, thoughts, and sensations to come up. She then began to pass her hand back and forth in a steady line at a specific pace and number of passes. On this first set, I heard a voice in my head, irritated and arguing that processing this was stupid. Oriana dropped her hand down the middle of the pass, ending the first series. I took a deep breath in and out. I reported what I noticed. Oriana told me this part was a protector who knew how to handle itself. She started the next pass and the irritated protector faded, replaced by a strong sensation in my chest. Oriana ended the pass and I breathed, reported what came up, and we began again.

The next pass showed me Paul and his incessant messaging, my mother never hearing me, and more disappointing visions of my father. Oriana ended the pass and instructed me to take a breath, and I reported back what had come to me. She nodded, "Go with that," and began the next set. This time it was more challenging to see images—all I could focus on was the intense feeling in my chest, like a dam about to burst. I told Oriana and she did another pass, quicker and shorter this time. The sensation eased and I could breathe. For the next pass, I was looking right at my father as he sat at the stove smoking, looking off into space, and somehow it was as though I could hear the thoughts in his head: *I'm not good enough, I can't do this.* I closed my eyes. Oriana stopped the process and gave me a moment to breathe. I came back to her and shared what I was experiencing.

"I'm ready," I said after a few exhales. Next, I saw myself, young, standing at the kitchen door and looking at my father, watching him lost in space, alone at the stove. I could also hear the thoughts in the young me's head, the beliefs she took in watching her father lost in himself: *I will do it all; you don't have to. No one is capable of helping. I can't trust.* There it was. Such a strange little memory, an experience that I had had countless of times with my father, and yet such a huge impact and shift in the way I viewed the world, would live my life. Oriana continued, beginning the next pass. Images of Marti and Janice came up. I exhaled, told Oriana. She nodded and took me into the next pass. I saw Adam and Magic D smiling at me with love. There was a warmth in my chest, a tingle in my hands. I exhaled. Oriana began the next pass. I saw Derek, Carol, and my lawyer, Susan. I felt strength in my chest, a lightness in my body, and the realization that I can trust, that I do trust, and that people are competent and can help. I told Oriana and she smiled.

A final pass, which was quiet this time. Oriana began to expertly close the session. "We'll come back to this place next session," she said as we contained the process using a beautiful technique called "a secure place" or a "calm place." In debriefing with Oriana, I was amazed at how I had been operating from two different systems of belief. It felt so good to be more whole, to have this integrated awareness and perspective. I could see how my trust in others and the support they offered were saving me—letting other human beings love me was restoring me. "Thanks," I called out.

"Ciao, ciao," she said, turning to make another cappuccino.

Fighter

My body was killing me. I didn't know why, considering I was still doing yoga and had even added swimming to my weekly exercise regimen. I brought this up to Oriana during one of our sessions, and she suggested I see Elijah, a colleague of hers and a gifted osteopath. I said fine, having no idea what an osteopath was but trusting Oriana that this would help me. Once I filled out the required forms and disrobed, as requested, from the waist up, Elijah entered and quietly placed his hand on my back at the top of my spine. He murmured to himself slowly and kept moving down, gently nudging and brushing his hand up and down and around.

"You have great fear of people touching you," he said gently. "Thank you for letting me work on you." My body melted into the table as I considered how I would recoil when anyone tried to bring me care. Elijah kept moving and said, "You dissociate easily." I murmured in agreement. He got to my sacrum and asked if I had had "a difficult entry into this world," if there were complications with my birth.

"I was three weeks late, an emergency cesarean section." He explained that he could feel the trauma in my body, that I had tried several times to be born rear end first, and the strain this had put on my back, not being able to push my way into the world. He opined that perhaps this is why I was afraid of touch, that I could not see the people before they tried to touch me, wasn't able to pass through the canal and see first.

I could feel him get quiet and carefully say, "I don't mean to make you uncomfortable, but you carry a lot of sexual shame, a lot of shame about yourself as a sexual being. Do you find that you are either hypersexual or, for the lack of a better word, dead?" I gasped. He was correct. I explained that I barely had a sexual relationship in my marriage, but in previous relationships, I had periods of high sexual arousal. He said he was working to have me in alignment.

After another moment of quiet, with some urgency, he asked, "Were you ever punished in dark corners or made to stand in dark corners?"

I told him I couldn't remember, but I seemed to carry a belief that I was bad and deserved to be punished. Elijah said, "Yes, you have a little one in a very, very dark place. No wonder you can't find her. You must help her now, tell her that you are here, she has you, and she is not alone."

I comforted myself internally, tears flowing. As I did this, thoughts came to me about how unsafe I was. I continued to tell this part that I loved her, that I—she—was almost thirty-nine years old, and we were okay now. After some time, Elijah released his hands from my head and back and said, "There, okay." He continued the rest of the session working on my legs, bending them, and not saying much else to me other than to murmur. Then he told me our time was over.

After I dressed and was preparing to leave, Elijah said to me, "You're a fighter and your body fights; it doesn't want to run." He was right, of course.

"I'm working on it," I mumbled.

"Why?" he asked. I blinked at him. "It's good to be a fighter. Even me, I fight and protect myself. I don't run." He said it with such peace, such confidence, and no wildness. I took that in. I mused that my fight had helped me survive, kept me safe, and brought me success. These days I was working on the choice of when to fight, not the skill itself, I supposed. I thanked Elijah and walked out into the cool air, hands open, no fight.

Cutting the Cord

Several weeks later, I received a voice call from John, the CAS worker. "Hi, Natasha, we need you to come into the office please," he said. "We have received some further information we need to investigate." The journal entry. I was sure of it. Paul had kept the letter in his back pocket and finally had sent it. Before I left, I sat myself down on my pillow and closed my eyes to meditate. Soon, an image appeared, and I saw a part of me, the young woman, the mother, wife, and daughter who had written that private letter to herself years ago, only to have it sent to strangers by a man who had betrayed her. This part of me was different than when I had first connected to her some months ago. She no longer looked exhausted or depleted. She was looking right at me, peacefully and calmly, the same way I was looking at her. She knew who her parents were. She understood the mistakes they had made and the boundaries she hadn't set, that she hadn't known how to set. I know now and she trusted that I knew now. Her arms hung to the sides, her hands open. "*Allow*," she said to me.

She began to soften back, and then I saw the image of Paul in front of me, strong and fierce, defiant. I looked at him, calmly, curiously. I could see clearly. This Paul believed he was protecting his children from a mother who was abandoning them. I could feel under his surface to his own exiled terror of being abandoned, perceiving me giving energy to myself as a rejection of the children and family, of him. I also saw the terror in his belief that the children were going to be abused by my family as I had been. He was so entrenched in this belief he didn't see it wasn't real. I sensed a part of me wanted to tell him to stop, to explain to him, to open his eyes to truth. I asked it to soften back, please, to allow, and it did. I saw it didn't matter what I said or what anyone else said. Paul would see what he wanted to see, just like each of us.

A thick, knotted cord was attached to his chest. I followed it and saw the other end was attached to me, to my chest. I had read about the cords and attachments we have with others. Janice had also referenced this in the Inner Sanctuary workshop, mentioning that we need to cut the cords in our lives that poison us. I thought about how I had consciously dropped my end of the rope in my tug-of-war with Paul, not realizing I had to go deeper, psychically cut the cord. I looked into Paul's eyes and then down at his chest to the thick coiled rope attached to it, the other end of the rope attached to my chest. I could feel the pulsing of energy in it flowing into me. It was fear, terror mixed with rage, resentment, anger, and punishment. I knew I had been feeding that to him as well, that the flow went both ways. I felt myself fill with light, the light and love I had been sending him for several weeks. I looked at Paul and said, "I am sorry, Paul, for all the poison I fed you. It wasn't yours; it was mine. I will not send it to you, and I will no longer take in poison from you." I visualized a white-hot blade in my hand and, grabbing the thick rope; I cut it, slicing it clean and watching it wriggle on the ground, retracting from me. The cord attached to my chest fell from me, my body restored.

"I hope you'll choose happiness," I said to Paul. "I hope Marie, or any woman you chose, loves you as you love her. Thank you for loving our boys. I love them, too. Be well, Paul. Goodbye." The image of him faded to blackness, and I sat with my eyes closed. I sat until my body told me it was time to stand and then walked out to my bicycle, making my way to the Children's Aid office.

Enough

I was sitting in a boardroom with John at a long table with twelve chairs, even though it was just the two of us. He had been paged to the front desk when I arrived, and we smiled awkwardly at each other on the elevator ride up. Sitting at the head of this long table next to him, I could see my letter. He flipped through the pages while he cleared his throat studying it. I could see all the passages highlighted, circled.

"Natasha," he began, "I had spoken to your ex-husband Paul about my investigation and that we were closing your file. He then produced evidence of concern and that is why you are here today." He looked up at me. I looked back at him evenly, calmly. "There are some serious allegations you've outlined here." He pointed to the folder and flipped back to page one. He began to read it aloud to me. After each passage I looked at him, calmly and evenly.

"You write that your mother and father exposed you to a child molester, they verbally and emotionally abused you, each parent had bouts of suicidality, and that as result of your upbringing, your sister specifically continues to be in crisis, and the list goes on and on," he said.

I continued to follow my breathing. "Yes, those are my words, and yes, these things happened," I said, "but forgive me, John, these things happened over twenty-five years ago. It's a little late for you to protect me from my childhood."

"Well," he said, "Paul's concern is not that your parents would emotionally or physically hurt the children. It's that they have no insight and would expose your children to this pedophile who is in your family. That your mother would take the children to visit."

"It's true," I said, "there was a pedophile in the family, and everyone handled it badly because of fear and generations of trauma. Understandably, my mother was a wreck when I was growing up, and my father was terrified and ran for cover when he didn't know what to do. My siblings found ways to cope in the short term that morphed into long-term problems. We all did the best we could, and I don't know any other family that would have done better given what we were up against. That letter you're holding tells a story of a family in pain, in need of help and care." I leveled my gaze at him and continued. "Back then, we didn't know how to do it, but I am doing it now, with my family, with my children." I began to feel the tears come up and I let them spill over. "My parents did the absolute best they could, and I'm proud of them, I'm proud of all of us because we made it through. And the love my mother has for my children is a gift to them. The role of grandfather for my dad is no threat to the children; it's not too great a responsibility for him to visit a few times a month. As you can see from the private letter you're holding, I have insight, I know what happened and see clearly where they went wrong and the choices I need to make for my boys." I folded my hands on the table.

John eyed me respectfully. "Thank you, Natasha. I appreciate that. However, this pedophile—"

I cut him off. "This pedophile moved to Portugal and died about a decade ago. If Paul is concerned about a dead, foreign pedophile, you should be making a referral for him." John smiled and quickly came back to seriousness. He began to read from the letter, but then slowed, scanned the page, and then looked back up at me. "I think that's enough, don't you?" he said and ripped the pages in half in front of me.

"Yes," I smiled back, "I think it's been enough."

Mirror

At my next session with Oriana, I wanted to explore the idea of being in a romantic partnership. After our months of work, we had processed a lot, but I was still concerned about losing myself again in a relationship and getting entangled in ways I never wanted to repeat. Oriana and I established memory and beliefs to target and then processed with eye movement. During one of the passes, I saw a guy I had dated before I met Paul and remembered how, after our second date, he left me on my doorstep and never called me again. At the time, it was painful and confusing, but with my new perspective, I saw this guy didn't like me much and he was done. That was it, no more to it. I giggled at the simplicity of it. I had the clarity that in relationships I don't have to analyze or figure out people, I'm under no obligation to work on relationships, and I can walk away if I want to. Oriana nodded, ready to continue.

Through the next few passes, I understood I was working through skills of discernment, of what I want and don't want, of letting go, and of moving forward. I took a deep breath and then exhaled slowly. *Discernment.* Something about that word hung in the air for me. I brought my attention back to Oriana.

As we moved forward, I recognized the loneliness I felt at not having more people in my life. Keeping myself safe came at the high price of isolation and its accompanying sadness. With the following pass, I heard a small voice from within almost whisper, *"Am I pretty? Am I smart? Am I talented? Do you love me?"* I saw an image of a young, desperate me calling out to Paul. The next pass, the image was no longer Paul; instead, I was calling out to my father.

Images and memories flooded my mind—my father, mother, Paul, and me, all in pain. I saw the sorrow and anger in these relationships. I saw how my behavior had hurt these people, how their behavior had hurt me, and the dance of abuse among us all. There was no blame in any of it, just grief and an acceptance of my part in it.

Oriana did a few more passes, and I received the knowing that all people are equal and all precious, and that all should treat each other as such. Then, it was almost as if a map of intimacy and vulnerability in relationships was laid out before me. With family and Paul, I saw each in their suffering, and that it was not mine to do anything about. My task was to be responsible for my reactions, emotions, and choices. Ultimately, the message was "Always come back to the love of yourself." By loving and choosing myself first, I made myself truly available to love other people in my life. I slowed down inside, and my breathing remained steady. Oriana signaled to me that the session was almost over, we were closing.

I thanked Oriana. She nodded and thanked me. "Ciao, ciao," she called after me as I headed back onto the street, back to my life, full of love.

CHAPTER XI

Special World

Paul had decided to rent a cottage for himself and the kids for two weeks in the early summer months, and I wanted to get away, too. Central America sounded ideal. I had been an avid backpacker before I met Paul, doing several solo trips in Europe and Southeast Asia. I decided I was going to Panama with myself.

I did some quick research and found a tiny village named Santa Catalina about a nine-hour bus ride from Panama City. I looked up a few hostels and decided to treat myself to a nice inn, ten dollars a night more than the ramshackle houses I saw. I was moving into my forties, and I wanted hot water and a bed, luxuries I could do without when I was young. This inn also hosted yoga retreats, though I was grateful to see that none were scheduled for when I'd be there. I wanted quiet. I did however email Lori, the woman who ran the retreats, and was thrilled to learn she was an expat from Australia who had married a local and moved to this remote village, where they were raising their son in the community. Lori wrote that she lived near the inn and would happily schedule a local teacher to come and lead me in some daily yoga in the pavilion amid the jungle trees, and her partner was available to give me surfing lessons, something I had always wanted to try. I gave her my dates, and all was confirmed.

"Your vacation is my nightmare," said my friend Laura as we sat on my porch the night before I was about to leave.

"What do you mean?"

"I'm not like you. I need people around and action. I need to be in the world," she said.

I smiled. "I've been in the world. I need to be in *my* world."

Panama

I had forgotten how terrible it was to ride these local buses, how many stops they made in remote villages and in places that made no sense to me. Streams of people, children, and animals climbed on and off, and I seemed to be the only one in it for the long haul. I smiled at the villagers, and they smiled back. I meditated, read, and took in the scenery, waiting for my stop.

Near the end of the ride, a fellow tourist got on the bus and sat nearby. "I'm Valentina," she introduced herself with an Italian accent. We chatted, both heading to Santa Catalina. She spoke Spanish, among other languages, and I said a little prayer of thanks for my new friend and translator, should I need one. It turned out I did. The final bus stop seemed to be in a remote area, not where the guidebook said it would be. Valentina barked at the driver, and he responded in a flurry of words, hands gesturing wildly. She looked frustrated, muttering curse words in every language she knew, including a little German. "Let's go," she said to me.

"Where?" I asked, grabbing my backpack from overhead.

"We're the only ones going to Santa Catalina," she said. "He said we can hire a private taxi from here."

"What?"

"It's a scam," she said. "They all do this. One of his buddies will show up in a car and charge the tourists on the bus a fortune to get us to where we need to go." Valentina continued to curse multilingually as we got off the bus, while the other passengers waited with little interest. I was surprised my body held no anger or fear. I felt grateful I had the money to be extorted. I was done fighting.

"We'll be okay," I told her. "I'm sure the money I pay this guy is going to go to better use than the four-dollar coffees and croissants I buy in Toronto. If you'll do the haggling, I'll pay for us."

Thankfully, Valentina accepted this idea, and I listened to another flurry of languages as she handed the private taxi driver a fistful of cash. She muttered to herself for most of the drive to the Santa Catalina Ecolodge she was staying at, but seemed to perk up when she saw her accommodations, which looked like some pieces of plywood nailed together in the middle of mud. With that and a big hug, it seemed like all was forgotten, and she waved as she walked away, calling out that she'd see me around the village. I smiled to myself, familiar with the shifts in parts and the moods that accompany them. Then the driver took me down the only paved road out of the village and dropped me at my inn.

"Hola. Natasha?" asked a beautiful young woman who introduced herself as Claudia. She spoke as I entered a modest outdoor reception area that preceded several bungalow-style rooms scattered about the area that led up to the ocean's edge.

"That's me," I said.

Claudia greeted me warmly and started the tour by showing me the yoga pavilion, which was right by the ocean's edge. She also waved to indicate a small dining area with a bar to the side and then led me to a cluster of rooms, telling me that the farthest one was mine, telling me with a bow to "Enjoy." I was a little confused about why my room, my own little bungalow with a hammock outside next to the front door, was away from the ones surrounding the resort, but I didn't really care; it was simple, clean, and perfect. I had a big wooden bed with a firm mattress and clean white sheets and a simple white blanket. A ceiling fan whirred above me, and the compact bathroom had an open shower with a stone floor.

Alive

For the next two days, I kept to myself, exploring the little village, with its one dirt road and two stores. I bought bananas and apples from the crates in front of the one store and a chocolate milk from the other, which served as a convenience store, stocking Kit Kats and bags of Doritos in flavors I'd never heard of. The little dining area of the resort had a restaurant, but I wanted to go into the village and eat at some of the restaurants that lined the main road. The food was outstanding. Even though the locals didn't speak English, Santa Catalina had quite an expat community of surfers and travelers who came to learn, and plenty never went back home. Although everyone was pleasant and friendly, I kept to myself, running into Valentina once or twice when she was hanging out with friends she had made. I was grateful the place I was staying at was far away from everyone, and walking the paved road alone in the dark at night was a comfort. I was amazed I felt so safe there, with the stars as my guide in a country I didn't know and a language I didn't speak.

Waiting for my first yoga lesson in the pavilion, surrounded by sunlit greenery, I felt strong and light. I was greeted by a lovely young woman who said little as she guided me to stretch my body and feel my breath, following the rhythm of the movements, the flow. It was amazing to be breathing in the humid air, stretching my arms high above my head, and looking out into the jungle where the pavilion was situated. It was quiet outside and inside my body. I took a moment to express gratitude to myself, to the part of me that cried on her mat in a yoga studio for the first time. Later that afternoon, still feeling peaceful after yoga, I was met by the equally quiet and sweet Sergio, Lori's husband, who had come to take me surfing. He handed me a long-sleeve water shirt to pull on over my bathing suit and motioned for me to get into his jeep.

When we got down to the shoreline, I was surprised to see the dark, rocky sand. It was not a "lie out on a towel and soak up some sun" beach. Sergio traversed the rocks and stones easily despite his bare feet, and with his finger drew the outline of a life-sized surfboard in the sand. He then lay down on top of it, demonstrating how to go from lying down to standing up quickly, how to land on your feet with perfect balance. He told me that I would need to learn this on land first, before I attempted it in the water.

I nodded and lay down on my sand surfboard, feeling foolish as I jumped up over and over. Sergio nodded each time I jumped up and took a surfer stance, mimicking what I had seen in the movies. He adjusted my form and had me do it again. After about thirty minutes of this, he motioned to the water, telling me I had good form, that I was strong from yoga, and that because I was small, it would be easier for me to be quick on my feet and low to the board. He told me he would paddle out the board with me, that this was the most taxing part for surfers. He wasn't kidding. When I tried it myself, I was surprised by how quickly I became tired, pushing over the waves, deeper into the ocean.

Once we got far enough out, Sergio told me to lie down on the board the same way I had on the sand, and that he would direct the board from behind, helping me catch a wave. He would then yell out to me when to stand and ride the wave in. "Okay?" he asked in his thick accent.

"Okay," I nodded back to him. I was shot through with adrenaline, experiencing it as excitement and buoyed by my naivete at what I was about to do. As I lay on the board facing the black beach, he got into place behind me, the soles of my feet at his chest, my arms spread out ready to paddle in unison with the wave. I could feel the ebb of the water, preparing for the flow of it to come underneath me.

"We go!" said Sergio as my board began to be pulled along over the wave. "Paddle, paddle, paddle!" I could hear behind me as Sergio pushed me along with the wave, letting me go with the water. "Paddle, paddle, paddle," he said as I moved my arms furiously in the surf. "And now!" I heard him cry out as I leaped to my feet and felt them land on the board, exactly where I wanted them to. They were only there a split second before I lost my balance and went flying backward, ass first into the ocean. I resurfaced quickly and beamed. I was a surfer.

Sergio and I stayed in the water practicing for another four or five tries, until I got up on the board and rode a wave all the way in. I whooped and hollered and squealed like a child, and I felt my whole body come to life. I had never felt anything like it. I was so un-self-conscious. I didn't care what I looked like or whether I was doing it right or wrong. I felt alive. It was incredible.

Yelling at Dad, Yelling at God

The next morning, I woke up to have a weekend call with the kids, and Paul didn't pick up. I was immediately furious. I tried to calm my body—it didn't make any sense to have this level of rage. I was happy to be away with myself, eating bananas, and the boys and Paul were probably having a lazy morning. These rational thoughts didn't seem to matter, and the anger wasn't budging. *Ugghh, really? After everything we've done, we're still going to do this?* I said to my parts. I knew I needed to move, that it wasn't a good idea to be isolated with this anger, so I walked out of my bungalow, barefoot, into the cool morning sunshine.

I headed down to the empty yoga pavilion and did a few Downward Dogs and Sun Salutations, and it seemed to quell some of the intensity of my emotions. But by 4 P.M., with no call back from Paul and the kids, no amount of yoga, sunshine, or surfing was going to satisfy the part of me that was angry at being alone. The anger threatened to engulf me and the voices in my head started in. I felt another part of me panic and I did not want to be overtaken by rage. I knew I needed to move faster, to run. I laced up my sneakers and scrambled for the paved road. I ran down the dirt road to the beach, along the sand, back to the dirt road, and then to the paved road, again and again, running up and down hills as different emotions and energies cycled through my body. I listened to all of it, witnessed it and experienced it. All of it was familiar, nothing and everything having to do with Paul. These feelings and beliefs I knew well. I had had them about my parents, my children, my friends. None of them were new. It was amazing to be able to witness myself in this way, how this system of mine interacted with the world in the same way regardless of different external circumstances. I had once heard that, as human beings, we don't experience the world; we just experience our own nervous system triggered by the world.

I was panting by the time I got back to the resort. I took myself back to the yoga pavilion. It was quiet, not a soul around. I was catching my breath when it began raining, a brief shower that had been threatening to roll through all day. I sat sheltered, watching the drops splatter on the gigantic banana leaves and wild vegetation all around me. I closed my eyes. I was tired of myself, and yet I was devoted to my healing and growing. The rain shifted from drops to sheets. The sky darkened and the wind picked up. I began to feel cold in my sweaty running clothes. I sat still and breathed, closing my eyes, and began meditating.

As I settled into curiosity, I heard that young voice in my head from my session with Oriana: "*Do you love me? Is it safe? Am I okay?*" I felt calm, curious, open-hearted toward this part, and ready to not just observe myself but to witness with compassion. I had been adding bilateral stimulation I'd learned with Oriana to my witnessing when I was on my own in meditation, tapping my left knee and then my right as I attended to my parts. This combination seemed to facilitate the type of experiences I was having when working with her. "*Yes,*" I replied internally, "*I'm here.*" This part was eight years old, and I could sense that she feared being *too much.*

I kept tapping, letting her feel my steadiness, that she wasn't too much for me, that I loved her, I saw her. With the next pass came a voice that I didn't recognize. "*I see you, Natasha,*" said the voice, so loving and so powerful that I bawled uncontrollably, shutting my eyes and weeping. This wasn't my voice. It was coming from inside of me, but it was bigger than me. I couldn't find words to describe the extraordinary feeling of love in my chest, radiating from my body. I kept tapping, wanting to be closer to it.

But then, there was a second voice. This one I knew. It was me at maybe thirteen years old—I could see an image of a young me seething with the anger I had been feeling in my body all day. I saw her yelling, "*Where are you, what are you waiting for, don't you see?*" She was yelling at her father, sitting at the stove smoking, lost in his own pain. This thirteen-year-old girl was desperate, screaming at him to look up, to help, to do something. "*It isn't fair, you can't just be comfortable while I'm suffering, while others are suffering, there are things that need to be done!*" came the screams.

And then she stopped yelling at her father, the image of him disappearing. Standing there, fists bawled tight, she was yelling at God. She yelled at God for all the times her mother went to church praying and crying for help. She yelled at God for all the depression and pain that consumed her father, robbing her of connection. She yelled at God for her little sister, lost in a downward spiral that started so early. "*Where were you? We can't trust you! Where were you when it all happened? When we needed you, you didn't answer!*" she yelled.

I kept tapping, kept breathing, witnessing in Self energy, and I heard that loving, powerful voice answer her: "*You were never alone. You've always been loved. There could be no interference. It had to unfold.*" There was such truth in that voice, such assuredness, yet such sorrow for all the pain it had to witness me endure. It felt like me as a loving parent to the boys, not able to interfere when I knew they were facing a challenge that was part of life, necessary for their development. And in that moment, I had clarity. This life journey, my history, had set the stage for me to truly know myself, to know what I was capable of, what I could overcome, how I could keep my heart open, and the depths of my love.

The thirteen-year-old girl stopped screaming at God and instead turned and hugged into my chest, and she felt me, the strength and resilience of me, the compassion and love I had for her, for all of me and what I had overcome. We had made it. We were okay.

Cascada

When the rain slowed down, I raced through it, squealing my way back to my bungalow. It felt wonderful to be running in the rain, my bare feet in the mud and grasses. A filthy dog sat on my porch, panting, clearly also just getting out of the storm. He came over and licked my legs, rubbing himself against me. I had just patted him on the head when I heard Claudia's voice calling, "Cascada, Cascada, Cascada?"

The dog barked.

"Over here!" I called out, matching Claudia's volume.

Claudia rounded the corner with a large, red umbrella, making her way over to us. She smiled at me with an apology in her beautiful, lyrical Spanish for the dog being in my space. "De nada, de nada," I said to her. "Cascada?" I asked her. "Beautiful name."

"Yes, yes," she said in thickly accented Spanish. "It is *waterfall*, Cascada is waterfall." My whole body tingled, and I felt a tenderness in my belly, a softness and grace.

I had four remaining nights scheduled in Santa Catalina before I had to be back in the capital to catch my flight home. All I could think about were waterfalls. I leafed through my guidebook and came across The Lost Waterfalls, which were situated in Boquete, a town several hours away from Santa Catalina, in the opposite direction of the bus ride back to Panama City. I knew it was my next stop.

With help from Claudia and the internet, I was able to set up a drive with a local tour service the next morning to get me to Boquete. Boquete was congested and dirty, definitely no Santa Catalina. It didn't help that it was pouring rain and gloomy. Looking up, I could see gorgeous, lush mountains and stunning vistas, but that didn't take away from the fact I was ankle deep in the mud and garbage that lined the sewer grates. I trudged through the throngs of people and made my way to the center of town.

I headed north. Soon, the busy street became sparse, and I continued west onto more residential streets. I found the bed and breakfast I'd booked and rang the bell. The couple who ran the place handed me a key and seemed busy, but I needed direction.

"Thank you," I said as I took my key. "If you could help me, please. I'm looking to go to The Lost Waterfalls tomorrow, and my guidebook recommends I get a guide. I'm pretty sure I can do it on my own, but I was wondering if you could tell me how to arrange a taxi."

"Well tomorrow is Sunday, so you'll have a tough time finding a guide, and they generally want at least two hikers or more to make it worth their while, but I don't think it's a good idea you do it alone. It's a three-hour hike and getting lost isn't the issue; it's falling and hurting yourself out there alone. Jerry?" she called out behind her. She and her husband discussed my predicament in German, and then he made a call to a tour company to see what might be possible. No luck.

"Oh, okay," I said, feeling foolish. "Thank you for your time."

I found my room, took off my pack, and sat down to think about a plan. Then it came to me. I scrambled back to the front gate and rang the bell.

The woman, annoyed, poked her head through the gate.

"I will pay the private guide the admission for two people if he'll take me," I said.

She looked over her shoulder and shouted again in German, her husband getting up and going back to the phone. In a few minutes, she let me know that Raphael would be there tomorrow to pick me up at 9 A.M. She said Raphael was a nice boy they knew well and would be a good person to do the hike with. She smiled tightly and wished me a good evening, shutting the gate firmly.

Let Me Do This

It was 9 A.M. and I waited with my backpack on at the front gate. Promptly, a car pulled up. Raphael unlocked the passenger door and I climbed in. "Hola," he said, grinning.

"Thank you for taking me," I said.

"Is no problem today," he said. "Excuse me. My English not so good," he said.

I smiled. "I should apologize; I have no Spanish. It will be a quiet day," I laughed.

"Quiet is good," he said. "In the quiet, you hear everything."

We drove in silence to the waterfalls.

Soon, we pulled up to a small fence, and Raphael parked, got out, walked over to a booth, and embraced the man sitting inside of it. He then instructed me to pay our fee, and we were waved through.

On our hike, Raphael pointed out eucalyptus trees and various mosses, specifically pointing out the invasive Spanish moss that threatened to destroy parts of the jungle. He had a wide knowledge of the vegetation and the frogs and bugs scattered across the wild. Although he often pointed things out and gave me details about their importance, it was indeed a hike with long periods of silence.

I climbed behind Raphael, who moved swiftly and expected me to do the same. We seemed to be the only people in the jungle this Sunday. "You move fast," he said to me, smiling.

"I do," I said.

"That's good, good. You have energy. Energy is good," and we kept hiking up and up.

It was truly breathtaking. It looked exactly as you would expect a jungle in the middle of Panama to look, and I marveled at the thick vines hanging off extraordinarily tall trees, the canopy letting in slits of sun that glistened over the water, which crashed over the boulders surrounded by more and more dense foliage. Little streams cut through the jungle floor, clean and clear and overfilled by the mighty waterfalls. I had yet to see them, but rushing water echoed all around, and I could feel the power of the falls.

"Come," said Raphael. "We go to Waterfall Two first."

Waterfall Two cascaded into a pool surrounded by rocks and enveloped by the opaque jungle. I held my breath and took in the splendor, the absolute perfection of nature.

"You swim? Go in?" asked Raphael.

"Yes, yes, can I?" I asked back.

He smiled. "Is cold."

"I'm okay. Cold is fine," I replied as I slipped off my shorts and shoes, bathing suit already on.

"I take a picture," Raphael said, miming photography. I handed him my phone and smiled in front of the deep pool as Raphael snapped photos. He placed my phone in the pocket of his shorts before he slipped them off and peeled off his shirt. He walked along the perimeter in his underwear and then plunged in headfirst. I waded in after him, the cold sending shivers up my thighs.

I dunked and swam, following my guide toward the break of the falls that thundered all around me. I couldn't get as close as he did, the power of the crashing water pushing me backward. Raphael laughed and clapped, applauding my bravery. We swam around for a few minutes, away from each other and to ourselves. Soon, I was getting too cold and pulled myself up onto a rock. Raphael came out a few feet away from me and sat on his own rock in silence. I could hear everything.

"Waterfall Three now?" he asked after a few minutes.

The climb to the third waterfall was more intense, and I had to maneuver over and under massive fallen trees and lush leaves and vines. In half an hour, we reached it. Waterfall Three was more powerful than the other and smashed into massive boulders, where the flow slowed. I was able to make my way across to the other side, stepping gingerly on large stones that led to a little makeshift perch. Sitting there, I could be close enough to feel the force of the falls safely.

I stared up at the majesty. I had never felt anything like it. The sun was so vibrant as it pushed through the clouds, and the deep multitude of greens all around me sparkled in the clear water rushing past the boulders and rocks at the base of the falls. It was incredible—the contrast between the mighty falls and the gentle water that moved at a distance from the break was breathtaking. I felt peace in the fast and the slow.

I closed my eyes and listened inside. I felt profound gratitude for being there, in that moment. I was grateful for my freedom, my strong body, my safety. Then I glimpsed an image of myself from before the divorce, a woman frightened about her future. Images kept coming: girls and women I had been in my life feeling frightened and unsure. I felt gratitude for them all, felt deep compassion and love for what they had experienced, what they had gone through, and how far we had come.

I saw flashes of the work I had done to arrive at this peace, all the healers and helpers who had supported my journey. Then I saw the young Paul, and the young me: girlfriend, wife, mother, desperately wanting to be loved and yet chasing, clinging, rejecting, fighting. Energy from this spectrum of memories swelled inside of me, potent and surging. I let it come, and with it, tears that spilled over. And then, as if they were coming from the falls itself, came rumbling words. *"I am more powerful than you. I am more powerful than anything. Let me do this."* I understood immediately. I had been led the entire time—the path had been laid out before me, and all I had to do was follow. I looked at the falls, bowing my head. I knew then that I wasn't alone, never alone.

Raphael had been waiting patiently for me, and we continued our trek in silence to Waterfall One. It was even more ferocious than the first two, and I spent my time there in awe of the greatness of nature and the beauty of all that was around me. On our hike back out of the jungle, we passed the first people we had seen all day, making their way to the falls, and they smiled at us. One woman remarked she couldn't believe Raphael and I had gone in the water, pointing at my bathing suit and Raphael's long, wet hair. "Was it freezing?" she asked.

"Yes, it was perfect," I smiled back.

CHAPTER XII

Return with the Elixir

On the flight back to Toronto, I looked over the pictures on my phone from my time in Panama. I smiled at the picture Sergio took of me beaming next to my surfboard. I was grateful that I had taken pictures of a restaurant I had eaten at, which had the most beautiful wallpapers and accent colors throughout the room, because I wanted to transform my own home from white and light to color and vibrancy. A slew of pictures came next that surprised me. Raphael must have taken them when he had my phone at the waterfalls throughout the day. There were dozens of them, of me walking into the falls, trekking up the hills, and looking off into the vine-tangled trees. One shot made me hold my breath. It was taken from behind me. I sat on the rock looking up at the falls. It was taken when I was hearing from God, that He had me. I silently thanked Raphael for this photo reminder.

Resurrection

I had been telling a friend and fellow therapist about my learnings from Janice, and she said, "Oh my God, you need to meet with Ruth."

"Who's Ruth?" I asked.

"She's no-nonsense. Some of us call her *the white witch* or *Ruth-less.*" She continued, "Really, Ruth is my go-to person when I need my butt kicked."

On a whim, I called Ruth, and she picked up, sounding startlingly nice. We spoke briefly, me sharing some of my spiritual experiences and explaining that I was looking for some mentorship and guidance about this new realm I seemed to be connecting with. "Let's meet and see what needs to be done," she said.

———

My first session with Ruth was scheduled on a day I had spent crying about being alone. I had gone online to look at dating apps, and my whole body recoiled at the concept. I knew that many of my favorite couples had met online, and it wasn't judgment I was feeling; it was heartbreaking loneliness and fear that I would never be in love again. I should have canceled my session with Ruth, not one part of me wanting any more therapy or to deal with my humanness.

I was meeting with Ruth to expand my knowledge and experience of spirituality. Unfortunately, I started crying within five minutes of sitting in the chair across from her.

Damn it, I thought, missing the past me that never cried and cursing Ryzio and Marti and Ken for breaking me open. I apologized to Ruth and explained briefly that I was divorced, was ready to start dating and be in a relationship, and was finding the process triggering.

"Oh, I see," she said, pressing me to go on. I tried to wave off her invitation to say more, wanting to direct the conversation to my spiritual growth, but the whole story of my past came blubbering out. Ruth studied me over the rim of her eyeglasses. She looked me up and down, pointing at something unclear, and said, "I see that in relationships you are dripping with need." My tears vanished and the soldier in me snapped to attention.

"No, I'm not," I said. "In fact, the issue in my relationships is that I didn't ask for any of my needs to be met."

Ruth shook her head, still looking me up and down and pointing at something. "You may not be asking with words," she said, "but your incredible neediness is pouring out of you and someone sensitive would feel it." She removed her glasses, took a tissue, and started polishing them. "Of course, they'd be confused by their sense of you, the disconnect between your neediness on the inside and the tough, independent, and practical you on the outside." She put her glasses back on, looked at me again from head to toe, and said, "You are dripping with need, and from what I can tell, most of it isn't even yours."

Again, I was confused.

"I get that," Ruth continued without waiting for me to respond. "A lot wasn't mine either. I had the whole holocaust on me," she said as she waved her hands over her body.

My first thought was this woman was nuts, and my second thought was she was mean. My friend was right: she was a white witch. Ruth continued, "And you're not really in your body. I don't think you've spent much if any time in there. How have you done all this training and therapy, and no one has addressed this?" She tsk-tsked and shook her head. "Or perhaps," she continued, "it's because you've done all this work that we'll finally be able to get you into your body. We'll see."

I sat up a little straighter, took a deep breath, and told her she was wrong. I was in my body. I could feel tingles and anger and sadness and grief; I could be held, and people could touch me. Ruth looked bored. I explained more clearly IFS, EMDR, the work with Adam, and all the meditation and experiences with God I was having. Ruth literally started bopping her head around, mocking me as I listed all the hard work I had done. I shut my mouth and stared.

"Listen," she said, "it doesn't matter what work you're doing. If you're not in your body, none of it means anything."

As I opened my mouth to tell her off, she said, "Do you feel your back against the chair? Do you feel your feet on the floor?"

I checked. I could feel the emotions in my body, but I couldn't really feel my body in the room. "Sort of," I answered.

Ruth told me to stop talking and "just sit there." Her voice got lower as she slowed down and said, "See if you can pour yourself into your toes. You are high up in your head. Breathe and pull yourself into your toes." I sat there, focused on my feet, which felt empty and hollow, and tried to drip into them. I immediately got scared. It was the most jarring experience to feel gravity pull me into my body. I resisted and then became angry, frustrated, and then scared again.

"What is all this?" I asked. "It feels terrible."

But I knew. I intuitively knew I was holding all the creepy, dangerous, slimy, painful, and abusive energy that I had absorbed throughout my life that was too unbearable for me to process in my youth. It's no wonder I wasn't in my body very much. Marti's words came back to me, that the cost of surviving my environment was a worthy price to pay, but the cost of still doing it was robbing me of my present life.

Ruth seemed to catch all these shifts and looked at me, telling me this is where we were going to start. "We're maybe looking at six months' worth of work," she said, writing in her notebook, "but hey, no promises."

Ruth-less

Several sessions in, I was sitting across from Ruth and silently trying to "pour" myself into my body. I had felt all sorts of horrible sensations I couldn't even describe. I sat there, looking at Ruth as she sat quietly looking at me, once in a while telling me to focus and come lower, deeper into my toes, ankles, shins, and thighs. It was hard work, and I felt various emotions flying through me, mostly vacillating between terror and rage. Terror at being in my body and rage at Ruth for making me. I observed all of it. When I got into my pelvis, the anger and terror shifted, and I felt a sadness and smallness well up. I began weeping quietly. When I felt like I had a handle on myself, when the emotion began to subside, I looked at Ruth and felt grateful that she had stayed by me, created a space for me to do this, and that I wasn't alone when I was finally in myself.

"Thank you, thank you for being with me," I said to her in a tender, childlike voice.

"Wha, whaddya say?" came her harsh reply, along with a screwy look. "I can't hear you," she said.

I found myself quietly smiling, suddenly loving this bitch of a woman sitting across from me. "I said thank you," I replied louder.

"Yeah," she said dismissively. "You say thank you and please a lot, you notice that?" she said back.

It took me several deep breaths and an eruption of emotion and tears before I could squeak out, "People haven't been very kind to me in my life," I said. "I guess I'm grateful when they are."

She looked at me directly and said, "You are the common thread in your life. You need to look at that," and I knew she was right. I was looking even deeper, deeper than spaces of victimhood, than abuse, deeper than the human psyche.

"I know I do," I said. "I'm working on really being here, in this body. I just haven't known how." She looked at me over her glasses, scanning me up and down with that same screwy look on her face, and then she turned to look at the wall as if she was listening to it.

Then I felt something shift in her, quite suddenly, and she looked back at me with almost tears in her eyes. "They're here," she said softly. "You have a room full of guides who have been waiting for you, specifically to help you be in your body. They've been waiting for you to ask," she said, taking off her glasses and wiping them. She was so tender talking about these guides, and I thought she needed one to help her interact with humankind. But then again, I thought it was the way she engaged me that caused me to listen. There I was, listening and inviting.

Boundless

It had been three months of working with Ruth, and when I walked in for our session, I was almost happy to see her. She sat in her swivel chair, swiping on her phone, and greeted me in her flat yet mischievous way. I sat and smiled at her, determined to sit with presence.

"So, what are we doing today?" came her matter-of-fact query. We'd spent all our previous sessions with me trying to feel my feet as I bawled, sitting across from her. I didn't want to do that anymore. I looked her right in the eye and began to talk slowly about my progress, how sending Paul love and light had me feeling more positive and peaceful, and how I realized I needed to start celebrating the healing work I'd been doing.

"Great," she said. "So, I can hear you talking from your navel. Now let's see if you can do it from lower down in your body."

I wanted to smack her. Instead, I maintained my composure and said again, "Yes, I know I can do more, but I see how hard I push myself, and I want to take a moment and really slow down and acknowledge where I am."

She continued to look at me with this disinterested, dismissive, thin-lipped face and said, "Okaaaay, but I'm here to push on the gas pedal and get you moving." I took a breath and chose not to bother explaining to her again I had been pushing myself for three straight years. Instead, I vowed to surrender myself to this white witch for the hour, silently tell myself that this was the end of the road with her—that I'd be sending her love and light for what she'd done for me so far, and I would be strong in my resolve that I was never coming back.

As the session proceeded, Ruth began to press me to be more present, to not look her in the eye but to "see" her, an important distinction she made. I felt myself wanting to, and that most of me could. And yet I sensed a sweet, beautiful, vulnerable little one inside of me, on my left, and my soldier, her protector, next to her, letting me know this white devil across from me could go to hell, and it would cut her down to size should she make one wrong move with a part of my most vulnerable Self.

Ruth kept nudging me with her murmurs as I sat there quietly, listening to this inner world. "So, can you see me, or are you afraid?" she asked.

I decided to tell her the truth. I knew that I could sit there, calmly and in peace, and I could speak for my experience, not from it.

I looked at Ruth and said, "You aren't kind or gentle, and I'm sitting with a part of myself that's vulnerable, that doesn't want to open up to you or anyone else that won't be tender." Ruth sat in her chair, her expression unmoving. But she was listening.

"I'm also listening to another part of me that is holding fear, but not for me, for you," I continued. "There is a lot of strength within me, a soldier that protects me and has the capability to destroy you with words should you push us the wrong way."

Ruth remained quiet as I finished speaking. We both sat in the room, feeling our backs against the chair, our feet against the floor. A few seconds later, she moved her gaze from mine and looked up at the ceiling and said, "Yeah, I'm not very gentle. My daughter was just telling me that."

I laughed, relaxing a little, but the soldier within me was still not at ease. Ruth continued, "What is it you're doing in there, with these parts?" she asked. "I have to say it sounds complicated and fragmented. From where I'm sitting, I see a woman, a whole woman, who is working to move herself out of pain and into her life."

I breathed, appreciating the simplicity of her observation and realizing how exhausting it has been trying to hold all the models, healings, and paradigms I had been experiencing. I appreciated the work with Ruth, sitting in the room, being with someone, and experiencing what is, all that is. I also could feel the fight still in me, calmer but there, the push against this power in front of me. I shared with Ruth what it was like to be with her, to want to push against the power in front of me at times, to feel helpless and misunderstood, to surrender and strengthen.

"Yes, our dance," she said. Again, how simple.

"Yes, our dance," I replied. I realized in that moment that I had so many different dances with so many different people. This was the one I had with Ruth, and she was staying, sitting in her own seat as I told her the truth of what was happening for me. I didn't have to fight her; she could hear me, and I could hear her. In that moment, I felt gratitude and love for her. I began to share with her how I had been sending Paul, my parents, and my siblings love and light. Ruth looked off into the distance, took a pause, and then said, "I'm wondering why you continue to go to gratitude and love and light instead of sitting with what I imagine is incredible grief for you when it comes to your relationships?"

How quickly my soldier cocked an eyebrow, flashing anger at Ruth's prodding. Simultaneously, I felt the grief and sadness about my family and Paul well up in me, pushing against my throat and chest with such force it almost bent me in half. I took deep breaths and felt all of it. When I steadied myself, I looked at Ruth and said, "I don't see the point in sitting in this sadness or grief in front of you," I explained. "I feel it when it comes up, and I have sat with it and processed it for years now. It is bottomless. I'm not ignoring it, but I'm confused at the rationale for sitting with it even more."

Ruth dropped her tone, softened her eyes, and said, "Can we change the word from bottomless to boundless?" And she was right: My love and sadness for the pain of humanity were boundless and stretched in all directions. They hurt my heart, yet were soft, tender, and full of love. I choked on tears and said, "It feels as if the love I have for my parents, the love for Paul, can't be felt. I've lost them, have no connection to them."

Ruth agreed, saying it was the intersection of love and loss, "all mis-steps," she called them, that have been in each of my relationships.

My heart opened to her kindness in that moment, the help. She continued, pointing out again that I was the common variable in these relationships, these *missteps*. I knew that Ruth and I had almost had a misstep moments ago in our dance. I could have pushed back harder, attacked her for not coming to me the way I needed, left the room, or given in to the thought that I would never come back, that I'd gone as far with her as I needed to. But instead, I stayed, trusted, and allowed, and then went deeper, to what lay underneath. I allowed myself to be seen in complexity and pain.

As the session ended, I thanked Ruth for staying and riding out the waves of the pushing, the soldier, and the vulnerability. "It's my pleasure," she said genuinely. "Don't you do that for your clients?"

I smiled and said, "I don't take clients as difficult as me."

"Yeah," she said, "but you're young. You stretch me. You will have those clients too, pushing you to grow."

I thanked Ruth and made my way to get my bicycle, vowing to walk it home and feel each step.

The Root

I was miserable as I walked into Ruth's office. I couldn't seem to get out of a terrible mood I had been in all day and was snarky and sarcastic with Ruth, wanting to match her difficult personality. After about fifteen minutes of sniping at each other, she stared at me exasperated and said, "Get on the table," motioning to a massage table against the back wall. We were coming on five months of working together, and for the last several sessions, I had been able to sink more into my body and feel the denseness of being human, the heaviness of walking around, and the weight of myself. As

I hopped onto the table, Ruth explained that we were going to get me grounded and pull my cords into the earth, securing me there on the planet and giving me access to its energy. Ruth pulled out a little pendulum and explained she was first going to assess my chakras. I hopped onto the table and obediently lay there with my eyes closed, waiting for my examination. Ruth started at what she called the *root chakra*, explaining that a chakra was an upside-down cone shape that spun clockwise, collecting energy from the earth, connecting to me at various places of the body. According to Ruth's pendulum, my root chakra—located at the base of the spine, the pelvic floor, and the first three vertebrae—was closed. "Not completely closed, but pretty tight," she specified.

"Why is it so tight?" I asked.

"Because you've been traumatized since conception," she lazily replied as she worked her way up my body, pendulum swinging. At my belly she told me this chakra was spinning in the right direction, "But it's wobbly." As she kept moving up, she explained that chakras either spin in the right direction, spin in the wrong direction, or move vertically. "They get confused," she said. She kept moving up and proudly proclaimed that my chakras were "All in the right direction, just all wobbly." I was quietly comforted, knowing all my healing work over these last few years had at the very least spun me in the right direction.

Then, Ruth held the pendulum over my throat and said, "Well, I've never seen this before."

My eyes flew open. "How long have you been practicing?" I asked her, concerned there was a new variation of chakra spinning.

"Since '92," she said.

"And you've never seen this! What is it?" I asked nervously.

"A magnetic force," she chuckled. "The pendulum came to a dead stop at your throat."

She was right. I put my chin down and looked over at the pendulum, and the thing was ramrod straight—a hurricane wouldn't have budged it. "What does that mean?" I asked.

"I dunno," she said with a shrug. "Let's get curious."

Ruth explained that the throat holds our taking in of nourishment and allows us to speak our truth. "Well, I know you can take in nourishment, so I'm curious if it's about you speaking your truth— even knowing your truth, the truth." She had a little sly smile, as if she was enjoying this mystery. As quickly as the smile appeared, it disappeared, and she said, "Okay, that's for another day. Back to the root," and moved back down near the pelvis. Or at least I thought that's where she was headed, but instead she came back up to my neck and shoulders and placed her hands on my body. "Let me know what you notice; you're sensitive, so you may really feel this," she said.

I did. I felt my legs come to life, and it was quite incredible. First, it was the left leg, then the right. I started weeping, tears of grief and welcome to my body. Ruth continued to go up and down my body, poking and doing other technical energy things. Once in a while she'd murmur, sometimes giggling to herself and other times sighing, but I lay there, tears streaming down my face, welcoming myself home. She spoke aloud that she was connecting the cords from my feet and perineum into the earth, and I felt the pull, the tug, and the connection to the ground. I continued to weep. When she was done, she looked at me matter of factly and said, "That's it for today."

Then she led me to stand in a squat and practice visualizing myself and the cords connecting me to this world.

It was past our session time together. I moved to gather my things, and asked Ruth what she had noticed in this strange type of spiritual surgery she had just performed. She looked at me and said, "Some of you doesn't want to be here and is resisting, but you really want to be here. It's not that you say you want to be here or think it. You really want to be here," she said seriously.

I looked at her just as seriously. "Yes, I do. I am devoted to being here."

"Well, good" was her reply as she turned around and returned to her seat.

CHAPTER XIII

Manifested

I t seems Janice was right: The desires in my creative lab and my meditations were beginning to manifest in the physical world. And it didn't happen the way I thought. I had been avidly looking online at real estate, found a realtor, and engaged in several bidding wars I lost. Friends and others told me I was "crazy" to think I was going to upgrade in the Toronto housing market at this time, and that I wasn't an ideal candidate for a larger mortgage, with my single-mother, self-employed status a barrier. I didn't waver. I knew I would get my house; I just didn't know how.

And then my mother called. "Are you still interested in moving, a new house?" she asked.

"Yes, I've been looking."

"Well, I know you have boundaries and don't like to get involved with extended family," she said. I was impressed that she saw me and was making efforts to connect with me where I was. "But a group of my cousins, ones you've never met, are looking to sell their family home, as their mother died, and I said you might be interested in a private sale."

"Yes, yes, yes, but why would they do that? The market is scorching hot."

"They are lovely people and well-situated financially. There are five siblings, and they are very close but would like the ease of selling the house. They don't want to deal with agents," my mother explained.

"Where is the house?" I asked, thinking there must be some catch.

"In the Annex, close enough to the boys' school, in a beautiful pocket of the city. Just so you know," she added, "the house needs a lot of work. It has good bones but hasn't been touched in sixty years."

"No problem," I quickly replied. "I know a contractor."

The Return

It had been three years since Trevor drove off from the townhouse. "Long time," I messaged. "I hope you've been well. I'm looking at a new house for me and the kiddos. It needs some work. Have room in your schedule?"

His response came in under five minutes. I remembered how Trevor and I had that ease with each other. We moved in the same way.

"Natasha, nice to hear from you, too. Send me the address. I'll take a look and see what we can do," he replied. Our exchange had me tingling.

The house was a shithole. I was standing in front of it, up the street from the coffee shop on Harbord Street where Trevor and I had agreed to meet. Even though it looked like a teardown, I stood in front grinning like an idiot, visualizing all the things it could be, would be. With a smile still plastered on my face, I walked into the coffee shop and ordered a chamomile tea, warming my hands from the December cold as I waited for Trevor. After a few minutes, I saw him out the window, walking back and forth in front of his truck, smoking a cigar and on the phone. He looked different from three years ago, rounder around the middle and tired. There was something comforting about him. I smiled. He gave me an awkward smile, pointing to his phone, motioning that he'd be in soon. I got up and ordered him a coffee, remembering how much coffee he used to drink. As I carried it over to the table, he walked in, shaking snow off his coat.

"That for me?" he asked as I slid the mug across the table to him.

"Hi, it's been a while, eh?" I stammered. I explained about the house and the sale price my cousins wanted, hoping he could give me an estimate of how much work it needed, cost, and timing.

"Okey dokey," he said. "Let's go take a look."

Trevor told me it was a big job and quoted me an exorbitant figure. My father told me, "It's a great price. It would normally be double, at least," so I agreed. I still hadn't figured out how to pay for any of this, but I knew this was my house, this was the next move. My cousins wanted to do the exchange by the early spring, with the closing in March.

Over the next three months, I worked with a mortgage broker who told me my best bet to get the financing done quickly was to remortgage my townhome and turn it into a rental property. Amazingly, everything fell into place. I found renters for the townhouse, charging them the rate I needed to satisfy the mortgage requirements, which was good for them and good for me. I was getting my house and trusting the Universe.

"I don't like it," Jesse said, when I took them to see the house.

"Yuck!" added Abe. They were eight and five. I couldn't believe how the time had flown by and how they had seemed to come into themselves, their personalities, and opinions autonomous from my beliefs and plans. The boys were not happy about the move, and they were even more displeased when they saw the dark, narrow hallways, cracked linoleum, yellowed walls, and cramped bathroom.

"I know, guys, it looks like crap"—they tittered at the word crap— "but it's going to look great because Mommy has something called vision. You'll see."

Jesse shrugged his shoulders and said, "I like our house now. It's cozy and so close to school."

I nodded. "Yeah, it's cozy and I like how close we are to everything, too. This will be a bit longer of a walk, but we can still walk and there will be a new neighborhood to explore."

He shrugged again.

"Abe, how do you feel about not sharing a room with Jesse? Having your own room?"

"What!" Jesse interrupted. "I'll have my own room?"

"Yes, honey, the back one upstairs, overlooking the lane."

"Cool, yeah. It's great! Can I pick my own paint color?" All of sudden, Jesse was excited.

I looked down at sweet Abe, visibly hurt by his brother's enthusiasm to not share a room with him. But he brushed it off and said, "Ha ha, I think my room's bigger than yours."

They would be fine. We were all going to be fine.

The World Shuts Down

Trevor and his crew began the work on my house the day before the province, the country, and the world shut down due to the coronavirus. Everything outside us was crumbling, yet my house was built in record time thanks to Trevor's resourcefulness and ingenuity in getting lumber and supplies during the province-wide lockdown. Miraculously, the house was completed on time, not a day over the projection, and I was coming along, too, feeling longer stretches of presence and calm, more sustained periods of experiencing joy and love. I felt love for my children, my clients, my friends, and for Trevor.

It started slowly between us. It wasn't the visceral knowing of attraction and want I had felt early on toward Paul. It was a comfort and calm when I was near him, and a quiet mind when I wasn't. I didn't have a preoccupation about him, which was a relief to me and a new experience with a man. I didn't think about where he was or whether he was thinking about me. I felt quiet on the inside and enjoyed his company. He had such a steadiness about him. We had been spending a lot of time together, both in person at the house during its construction and on the phone while planning out materials and schedules. These work meetings really only warranted ten minutes, but we let them stretch into hours. He would sit on a pile of two-by-fours, puffing on his cigar as I told him stories about my day for the pleasure of seeing his eyes dance and hearing him call me "delightful."

Three months after the start date, as the renovations were wrapping up, I began to see him differently, sense him differently. He was a big bear of a man, towering over me in height and thick with strength and life experience. He didn't talk much about himself or the past at all, which was initially no problem as I'm a chatterbox, but I noticed with my slowed nervous system and more sustained presence that I was curious about him. Not for the purposes of understanding him or "figuring him out," but simply because I wanted to know more about the human being in front of me.

He had told me that he was sober and had had a serious drug and alcohol problem in his past. He'd also shared about some of the volatile relationships he had been in with women who had been wildly erratic and abusive toward themselves and later to him. I knew he was adopted and his biological mother was First Nations, fifteen years old at the time of his birth, and unable to care for him. He'd told me her life had been unstable, and she had dealt with a legacy of trauma handed down to her by her own mother, who had been raised in residential schools and carried the darkness of her time there. I knew she had courageously and with love put him up for adoption to a family who loved him and provided him with stability and care throughout his drug-fueled and chaotic early life. That early life seemed so discordant with the calm, serene man who puffed his cigar in front of me.

"Trevor?" I began my sentence carefully.

"Yeah," he said.

"How do you understand it? You moving away from abusing crack, alcohol, prison, and the relationships you were in. How did you get from there to here?" I asked, sitting next to him and taking a puff from his cigar.

"Oh, why do you want to know that?" he said. "It's irrelevant. I'm in the present, right here, enjoying sitting with you."

"I know," I said, enjoying the smell of his cigar. "I'm curious how you did it, moved from so much pain and chaos to here."

He took a moment, and I could sense that he was deciding whether he was going to make a joke and brush off the conversation or whether he would truly answer. He looked up at the sky and lifted his huge arms and said, "The Universe."

"What do you mean when you say Universe?" I asked.

"I only know what it is to me, my dear," he said. "And for me, it is everything. I had to get out of my own way and surrender, trusting the Universe knew the better way for me than I did. I had my chance, and I messed it up pretty good. This way is better," he said, taking his cigar back from me.

"But how did you do it? What did you have to do to get there?" I told him a little about all the processes, the work I had been doing to get to this space.

He rolled his cigar back and forth in his hand and told me about his history in multiple rehabs and hospitals from overdosing, as well as one serious, drug-induced psychotic break. One day, it had been enough, and he made his way to AA. "It was the twelve steps," he said. "If you follow them as they are simply laid out and you really do the work and commit, you give yourself to your higher power and the whole Universe welcomes you and guides you," he said seriously.

In the ensuing weeks, our conversations deepened and I learned about Trevor's devotion to prayer and meditation, how he led his life and made decisions by asking himself if his choices were loving to himself and others. I learned he wasn't motivated by money, but rather by service, creating homes and comfort for his customers and jobs for his employees. I learned of his integrity and courage, and I came to love the *reliability*, *predictability*, and *consistency* of a man who knew himself and trusted his God, his Universe. With Trevor, I co-created a relationship where I could be met in my sovereignty and meet him in his.

The Slayer

Toronto had shut down quickly, along with my sustained periods of peace and calm. I scrambled to move my clients online, no easy task for a technological dinosaur like myself. But then the schools closed and the kids were home. It was incredibly challenging to juggle my attention from online trauma sessions with my clients to the support Jesse and Abe needed to stay engaged in virtual learning. The boys and I had talked several times about what is and what is not an emergency when it came to disturbing me and my work. Abe especially was slow to understand that wanting to buy a new video game was not an emergency. Being thirsty was also not a knock-on-Mommy's-door emergency. I introduced my sons to the sink and the drawer with the cups. On one particular day, I had asked my mother if she could be with the boys for a few hours, as I had a tough day scheduled, including multiple clients who were working with complex trauma. I asked her specifically to come before 10 A.M., as that was when I would be starting my online sessions and could not be disturbed.

That morning, I didn't hear from her. Normally, I would call and triple confirm, but I was working on trust and not being controlling, so instead I felt anxious and stared out the window. At 9:55 A.M., I traded anxiety for rage and called her incessantly. No answer. I loaded the boys up with water, snacks, and their iPads, and told them again not to come upstairs unless it was a real emergency and to let Nana and only Nana into the house. I went upstairs, smoothed back my hair, and logged on to see my client sobbing into a towel. I needed to focus on our session. At 10:18 A.M., in between my client's wails, I could hear my mother's excited voice riling up the kids downstairs as she arrived late. Jesse exclaimed, "Flowers! Mommy loves flowers!" and then little feet were stomping up the stairs toward my bedroom/office. *He won't, he wouldn't dare,* I heard my internal voice say as the outside me nodded along with my client's pain. I began to panic as I felt rage course through my body, afraid of the holy hell my soldier would unleash on Jesse if he came to the door.

But his little knuckles knocked on the door. *Don't do it, don't do it,* I pleaded with myself, but it was too late. I smiled tightly at my client and asked her to give me a moment, and then hit the mute button and turned off my screen. I turned around and ripped open the door with the fury of a cage fighter and faced my precious eight-year-old son, who smiled widely as he thrust a bouquet at me. There was nothing I could do to contain the rage. I watched, helplessly trapped inside my soldier, as I snarled at him and threw the flowers aside. "I'm sorry, Mommy," he whimpered, a sensitive child shattered by my reaction and how he had upset me. I slammed the door in his face and tried to breathe through the fire in my body while my heart shattered and I plunged into shame, my dance with myself.

I somehow got through the session and was grateful to see my next client had canceled. At the same time, the empty hour gave me time to be with myself undistracted. I stayed in my bedroom with my rage, terrified to go downstairs and abuse my family members. I closed my eyes and tried to meditate. When that didn't calm me, I tried the Inner Sanctuary and punching it out in the gym. No dice. I was breathing deeply, pleading with my anger, my soldier, not to overtake me. I tried to override it by putting on my running clothes, telling it that I was going to jog my body out the door and if it wanted to destroy something, it could shred the pavement and give me a good workout. Just please don't say anything to my mother. Please don't engage anyone downstairs. My soldier laughed in my face.

I ran down the stairs, feeling like Sigourney Weaver in *Alien*, holding this beast within me, trying to keep everyone around me safe. My mother looked up at me like an innocent puppy and asked, "Honey, is everything all right?" I pivoted as I was reaching for the doorknob.

BOOM.

"Just what did you think would happen when you showed up late in the middle of my session?" I snarled. Jesse ran by me out the door and crossed the street, hiding behind a tree. Abe stayed at the table, coloring and eating Doritos, blocking out the venom hurtling past his sweet head toward my mother. My mother appeared clueless before me. Realizing that I might burn the house down, I took one more giant push to get myself away from everyone, burst through the door, and started running down the street. *Anchors, all anchors*, was the mantra streaming in my head and then out into the world. Once the adrenaline had released from my body, big, fat, rolling tears came and I silently pleaded with the humans in my life, *You don't need to help me. Just don't make it harder for me.*

I felt I had been trying so hard these last few years on my own. I had pushed through the separation and all the ugliness of the divorce, pushed through huge healing journeys and navigated shadows and pain. I was finally in a place where I felt safe and solid enough to ask for help, and there I was screaming at a house full of people over eighteen minutes and a bouquet of flowers. I was deeply ashamed. Finally, I stopped running. I sat under a tree and let my body sob and shake. I couldn't do this anymore; I couldn't let this soldier take me over like this. I saw an image in my mind's eye of my tiny Self running around the world trying to hold everything up and God's voice saying "*Silly girl, let me do this*" and "*I am more powerful than you. I am more powerful than anything.*"

After my breath evened, I limped back home, silently walked past my family to my computer, and canceled my afternoon clients. I went upstairs and sat in the shower for a long time. I toweled off and said goodbye to my mother and gave the children the TV remote for the evening. "Mommy?" came Abe's voice up the stairs. "Mommy, Trevor's here."

I wasn't expecting him, and I was in no mood for company. "Where the hell have you been?" he asked as I came down the stairs. "I've been trying to call you."

"Hiding," I said, as Abe pranced back to his show.

"Hiding? Why?"

"Because I'm a monster and I lost my mind on everyone, so I need to hide myself away."

"Okay, well, I think that's stupid," said Trevor.

"What?" I asked.

"I said I think that's stupid. Just tell me what happened. We don't need all this drama."

I sucked in my breath, waiting to feel a surge of rage at being called dramatic, but it didn't come. Instead, I blurted out the whole story like a little kid that had just shoplifted and told him how bad and horrible I was, all the ways I had damaged Jesse and Abe and set myself back with my mother. When I finished, I waited for Trevor to tell me all the ways I could have managed this better and how I'm working too much and too stressed and need to slow down.

Instead, Trevor looked at me and said, "Well, you're trying to run a goddamn business from your bedroom during a pandemic. They need to understand your time needs to be respected."

I was stunned, actually stunned. "What?"

"I said that was bullshit. There is no reason to show up at that time, rile up the kids, and disturb you. If people are going to help, they should help and not make things more difficult for you. And Jesse, well, he does know better and needs to think."

I had to sit there for a moment and take it in. Trevor then looked at me and brushed the hair out of my eyes, gave me a kiss, and said, "Okey dokey, we okay now? Let's get you a cookie," and walked over to the kitchen.

I sat, dumbfounded. He had reinforced I had needed help and support and not another obstacle. He didn't shame me for my behavior. Most importantly, he made it clear I didn't have to destroy myself or anyone else in the process. *Okey dokey.*

Trevor took the boys out for ice cream to give me some space, but I knew I had to look at this rage, this soldier. I composed an email:

Hi, Janice,

I hope you've been well. I've been doing my Inner Sanctuary, and I'm in the house I manifested in my Creative Laboratory. But I'm hoping we can have a session together. There's some energy I want to explore. I fall into this place of wanting to destroy everyone around me and give away my children. No big deal, right?!

Thanks, Janice.

Love,

Natasha

I received her response the next day:

Okay, then. Mass destruction and giving away children. Nope. No big deal. All I can say is it's about time to face this music. If you have recognized this behavior before, then the intensity is demanding to be healed.

We arranged a three-hour session, and I exhaled.

As Above, So Below

Our appointment day came, and it was time to *face this music.* I kissed Trevor goodbye as he left for work, joking that he was going to come back to a girlfriend with a spanking new personality. He replied that was fine, but I secretly thought he was worried. Trevor was part of a rare breed that gets out of his own way. He had been meeting my friends: Philip, Suze, Mark, and Bianca. He listened as we talked about Ryzio, the Inner Sanctuary, and psilocybin journeys. At one point Philip looked at him and said, "What do you think of all of this we're doing? How does it sound to you?"

Trevor took a haul on his cigar and politely said, "I don't know much about what you're talking about. I guess I wonder when is it done, when is it enough?"

We were all quiet—we'd never really thought about that. When do you just live? Trevor was living. He told me he wakes up every morning and tells the Universe he will do his best throughout the day to get out of the way. He asks for guidance and hears the same thing every morning: *Be helpful, be kind, be loving.* Then he goes to brush his teeth. He is a very good man for me. He is a very good man.

So, he roared off in his truck, I finished my last cup of coffee, and soon it was time. I set myself up in my bedroom and waited for Janice's presence to enter via Zoom.

"Can you see me?" Janice's voice came through the computer audio. *I love this woman.* "Hi, Janice, I'm here, I'm here. Can you see me?"

"There you are!" she said, delighted. We greeted each other with our hearts, our souls. Having Janice greet you with her heart and soul was always such a wonderful feeling. "Hi, baby," she said. "Are we ready to do this? Are you really ready to give up the power this rage has given you?"

I took in her words and got quiet. "No, I don't think I am," I said truthfully. "I like this power. Honestly, it kept me safe as a child, got me out of my marriage, and has helped me navigate the world. I am successful because of it, fearless because of it."

Janice's eyes twinkled. I think she was surprised and glad for my honesty. "Ah, yes, power," she responded. "You think this is power. In many ways it is, but not the type of power that nourishes you, propels you in the direction of love and wholeness. This power will only destroy, it will destroy you. You decide, you choose," she said.

"I want to hold on to my fearlessness, my power, but not in the way that destroys. I don't know another way," I said.

"It is true, you have operated this way as the soldier, the slayer, and you are conditioned. You must see how this slayer has hurt you, hurt those around you."

I thought about poor Jesse's little face as I threw open the bedroom door and snarled. I thought about Paul and the way I used to destroy him in our fights. I thought about my mother, how vicious I could be. "It's tricky, Janice. I can see how this slayer energy hurts and abuses, but at the same time I see how people in my life have harmed me, crossed lines with me, and I'm protecting myself."

"Yes," she said, "this is tricky energy. It feeds on the illusion of victimhood and calls you to join cycles of pain, shifting you from abuser to victim, and round and round you go."

I saw the drama triangle that Marti had taught me. I saw all the untangling I had done, all the healing, and how I had gotten caught up in it again. Yes, this was tricky energy. "I guess I'm scared to be without it," I said, "scared that without my fearlessness, I will be weak."

"It is your fearlessness that is causing you to head into danger," Janice said. "How else can fearlessness show itself if it is not attracting danger?"

The truth of this shook me.

Janice continued, "We need to mature fearlessness, heal it, and transform it into courage, wisdom."

I watched her face, trying to imagine doing what she described but feeling wary about the undertaking.

"Reflect on how courage and wisdom have served you and contrast it with fearlessness and this slayer power. What are the outcomes you create from your choices?"

With that, I was ready to see this slayer, this soldier.

Janice asked me to lie flat and get comfortable, close my eyes, and we would begin the "induction process." She instructed me to breathe, slowly and deeply, relaxing my body. I could hear her beautiful, strong, yet gentle voice inviting me to notice the softening and relaxing of my legs, my belly, my chest, neck, and head, to relax my arms, fingers, and toes. Just let them go. Janice continued, saying I would see a stream of light, and from that light a golden ball would descend and land at my feet. "Tell me when you see the ball, when you feel it," she instructed.

I did. It was soft and gentle, like a bubble coming down and sitting at my feet.

"Wonderful. This ball will now enter your body and travel up your legs, torso, all the way up to the top of your head, nourishing you with its golden light and love."

I felt it. I saw it, golden rivers of light tingling up my body and filling me completely with peace and love. The ball exited out the top of my head and Janice said, "Thank this ball for nourishing you with its love and guide it back into the light, up, up, up, back to the light. Send it home with your love."

I did. Then I saw another golden ball, smaller than the first, coming down from the light toward the crown of my head. "You will see another ball descend," said Janice.

"I already see it," I said.

"This ball will hold all the thoughts you don't need right now. All the planning and all the worry: watch them go into the ball for safekeeping. They will be returned to you at the end."

I watched as my thoughts seemed to float from my mind, absorbed into this ball, and the weight was lifted from me. Again, Janice instructed me to send this ball back up into the light, thanking it for its service of safely guarding my thoughts. She continued, "From this relaxed state, I want you to imagine breathing in light, the nourishing light of the Universe. Now," she continued, "as you exhale, you are breathing that light back into the room. Light in and light out, you are surrounded by light."

I was floating in light. It supported and held me. "You are expanding, lighter and freer, freer and lighter," she said. I felt myself rising up as she said I would. I found myself floating upward, out of my body, out of the house, up into the sky, and entering the cosmos.

Janice instructed me to look at my hands, to look at my body. I saw hands of light, a body of light, my light body. I felt wise, I felt love, I felt gentleness and strength. "This is you," said Janice, "this is who you really are." I felt the truth of that, *who I really am*, this love, this light.

I found myself hovering high above the planet and looking down and seeing what looked like Egypt, thousands of years ago. I was drawn to a specific man, bloodied and defiant, on a line of broken men pulling large ropes, constructing cities and pyramids. I intuitively recognized that man as me, me from a past life. I told Janice what I was seeing and she murmured, validating that I was seeing what I was seeing. She said, "What are the thoughts in that man's head?"

I watched the anger and rage on his face, the flashing in his eyes as he was being whipped and forced into slavery, building for men he did not honor. In his head, I heard, "*I am more than this. To them, I am nothing, I am their tool, used and taken advantage of.*" His thoughts and his energy melded with my own about being used, not seen, taken advantage of as a wife, a mother, a therapist, a daughter. How I felt and knew that I was more. I saw how these thoughts and this rage exploded out of my body and could cause great harm to me and those around me. I started weeping at the realization, the understanding.

I heard Janice say, "You have turned this rage into an art form. You have had thousands of years to perfect it and now you are back, back to the Source, back to heal it."

I nodded through the tears. Then I heard from within me, "*This seed, this anger, it is nothing but destruction and pain. We release it now, back to the light, back to love for transformation. The seed of light and love is within you,*" this internal voice told me. "*It will nourish you and bring peace, strength. Everything outside of you isn't real, none of it is real. Only this love and this peace inside of you is real.*"

I looked back at the man on the line, caked with dust and blood. I looked at him in his suffering and could hear the thoughts in his confused head, that he had no way to feel peace and love in his heart when all around him was death and destruction. Then I heard, "*All that you see outside of you isn't real, none of this is real, none of it. All is illusion.*"

I reported to Janice what I was seeing and hearing. She directed me to take a seed of light into my light hands and place the seed inside his heart. I did and then stood back, watching the light fill his heart and every chakra in his body. I watched as he rose. He breathed deeply as the light spread throughout his body and his flesh expanded, turning his damaged body to muscle, smooth and strong. And with that transformation I heard him say, "*I will make the best pyramids. I am devoted to doing my best work.*" In that moment, he made the choice to direct his energy and focus away from his circumstances and instead to the creation of these great structures, using the fullness of his strength, pride, and determination. The environment also began to shift and I witnessed as he no longer focused on his abusers but instead on caring for his fellow men, sharing kind words of love, encouragement, and peace. He dedicated himself to their service, bringing them solace, soothing them, and showing them the way to peace. While simultaneously, I felt his hope for more, his hope for advancement, for freedom, and the expression of the life he dreamed for. Importantly, I felt his patience, his knowing the external world would shift, change. He would have his freedom, but not by destroying, not by abusing himself and those around him. That for this moment, this present moment, he would choose love and peace.

Return to Love

"How does this man live within me?" I asked Janice at the end of the session. She explained that human beings have come to earth to know themselves, individually as part of the collective. She drew a diagram starting with "The Monad," the Oneness of love, peace, and wholeness. She said that to know ourselves, we choose to come to earth to fully experience and restore ourselves back to that wholeness of love and peace. Part of that process involves descending into denser and denser matter, which results in the forgetting of who we truly are, which is peace and wholeness. Instead, we become the individual, confused and disoriented, fearful of the other and our new aloneness and vulnerability. To *know yourself* was the same message I had received internally, out in rain under the pavilion at Santa Catalina.

"You see how this man lost his way," Janice continued, referring to my process. "You see how you have offered that part of yourself, developed thousands of lifetimes ago, a pathway back to remembering, back to wholeness, to healing."

I felt tingles up and down my spine. "But help me understand how someone like Trevor just gets it, how he was able to surrender to his higher power and didn't have to go diving and healing all the trauma?"

Janice smiled and said, "Honey, you don't know how many lifetimes he's worked through to be able to do that. Focus on *your* journey, your path. All people are here to do their own work their way. Don't invade them, don't pull them onto your path. Trust that they'll find their way—or they won't, and that's fine, too. We all do it in our time, and time is eternal."

I could see how each painful life experience the people in my life had had, each knock to the ground, was an opportunity to go inside, to heal what was calling out to them. I wouldn't interfere, but I also wouldn't participate in the cycles of pain. I could hear Janice's words imprinting on my heart: "We are all here to remember and return to love."

CHAPTER XIV

Adventure, Discernment, Creation

After my session with Janice, the world opened up for me. I found gentleness in my quiet moments with the boys, I felt trust and support in my relationship with Trevor, and I felt warmth and gratitude toward my parents while maintaining boundaries that felt right for me. I continued to meditate, do yoga, and connect with my new community of friends who all supported and encouraged each other to get curious when hijacked by emotion. I recognized that my work with Ruth was done and she agreed. I was ready to live and experience from the present and work with the past as it came up. My private practice was thriving and I was teaching from my experience and supporting others on their own healing journeys. My co-parenting arrangement with Paul wasn't always smooth and it wasn't always easy, but I navigated it from a place of clarity about who he was and where he was stuck in his limited insight and perceptions based in fear and anger. I didn't know what life would look like for him, but I was no longer going to attach my peace and life experience to him and his choices.

Then one day, in a meditation, I thought of Magic D and my mushroom journey with him. Almost two years had passed. I couldn't quite put my finger on it, but I felt called to do another journey, remembering what he had said to me when I left his home: "Next time we will open your heart to you, to self-love." I recalled that he had said something about using MDMA and not psilocybin, and even though I was curious, I was not interested in synthetic drugs, especially after talking to Trevor. Given his decade-long battle with cocaine, crack, and booze, his opinion was that "any use of chemicals is stupid," especially when it came to connecting to God. In our discussions, he kept asking me what my intentions were and then said, "When is all this inner stuff done? Just start living." I listened to his points, knowing he had my best interest at heart, but also knowing I had a feeling—I couldn't quite explain it but I kept thinking about it, and it got stronger day by day. I was surprised that Trevor had a difficult time accepting my reasoning, that I had a *knowing, a feeling about it*, as this was how he directed his life. "I feel called to see Magic D," I told him. "I can't explain it."

MDMA

On the day of the journey, I left my bicycle at home and took the subway across the city. I knocked on the door, and Magic D greeted me with his sweet smile and warm hug. As we sat together and caught up, he grinned like a peaceful monk, hands clasped in his lap, shining his presence on me. I confessed, "Actually, I'm pretty scared about today's journey." He told me he was glad I felt some fear because this showed I had respect and reverence for the unknown. He said he worried when people showed up arrogant, with confidence to conquer the unknown, instead of with courage to see and experience what the teachings would offer them. He said these medicines, these tools, are powerful, and they are gifts to us—and like all powerful gifts, they can also be dangerous if handled without wisdom, just like fire. We talked about how more people who were searching for "spiritual experiences" were experimenting with drugs, and he explained he worried people would get hurt if they ventured into the unknown without an experienced person not only guiding them, helping them navigate the experience, but also helping them to integrate the healing journey with the Ego structure afterward. He concluded, "People need to remember that the medicine isn't here to make you feel good. It is here to show you what you need to heal."

Self-Love

It was time to set an intention and begin the ceremonia. As before, Magic D had me select cards from his deck. I pulled Adventure, Discernment, and a blank-faced image. Magic D smiled and said, "Out of seventy-two cards in this deck, there is only one blank one. It is a special card." Then he rubbed his hands excitedly to begin our journey with *Adventure, Discernment,* and a *Blank.*

We headed upstairs, and as before, we meditated.

Magic D blessed the space with tobacco and said a few prayers in Spanish. He then blessed the capsule of MDMA in a bowl, handed it to me, and directed me to set my intention and to thank the medicine for its assistance on my journey. I swallowed the capsule and headed to the chaise lounge next to the speakers, and Magic D handed me the goggles and covered me with blankets, giving my arm a squeeze and wishing me well.

I closed my eyes, took a deep breath, and waited. Some time passed and I felt nothing. I thought I might need to ask Magic D for more. Instead, I followed my breathing, watching my thoughts come and go about Trevor, the kids, my work. Then I felt it. The music in my body, a strange sensation. Each note felt like a twinkle exploding within me. It was pleasant, at first, and then I felt myself annoyed. It was too much sensory experience, although I did like the feeling of breathing full inhales and the peace that it brought me. I focused more on the pleasure of breathing deeply and how good the tobacco smelled in the room. More music notes moved through my body as I felt myself slip deeper into the experience.

Then came a feeling of falling and a pulse of panic as I clung to presence, not wanting to enter the unknown. Instinctively, I talked to myself with love and gentleness: *"Everything is okay. Thank you, Ego. I'm going to separate for a little while but I promise I'll come back."* And with those words, suddenly I had full clarity. I didn't want to relinquish my Ego, travel to the cosmos, and experience full surrender. I was here, ready to live. I was done with today's journey—I had arrived.

I sat up, took off my blindfold, and told Magic D I was done. He looked surprised yet accepting, welcoming me to come sit with him in the ceremony corner and talk. I got up shakily; I was high as a kite but very clear. Physically, I felt like shit, not liking the feeling of this drug in my body. I lay on the floor while Magic D perched on his meditation pillow across from me, and I talked of what I'd learned. But it wasn't talking; it was channeling. I could see and feel the truth of the learning as it was formed into words and shared with myself and Magic D, like a gift of knowledge coming through me:

> *We're not here to be Egoless. We're not here to separate from the Ego and live a spiritual life. We need the Ego to live a human life, a life of adventure and a blank slate to create whatever we want. We are to use discernment in life's creation, to determine whether we are creating our life from the trauma embedded in the Ego. That is why there is crisis in life, because the Ego was separated from the spirit and went its own way*

through its own power and operates from its trauma.
It's this trauma that blocks out the love and wisdom
available to us, inherent in each and every one of us.
It is only when we surrender the way of the Ego and
heal the lens of trauma can we be led by the divine.

In that moment, I understood what Trevor was talking about. The twelve steps, surrendering to a higher power, and forgoing the messages from his Ego was his path. My path was to go through the Ego. I was choosing to heal and restore my Ego, my parts, and partner with it. As I relayed all of this to Magic D, a rush of gratitude and love for the human experience filled me and gentle tears rolled down my cheeks. "This is the gift," I said to him. "The gift to all of us is our unique personality—for me, the gift of the personality of Natasha. The gift is Natasha to create whatever I want in this life and have the Spirit guide me in its creation. That's my birthright if I will accept it. My soul will get what it needs from the experience and the gift is my human life and all its potential."

I breathed that in and integrated the truth that my life was an adventure to be lived as I chose, not to be sacrificed for my soul to get the experience it needed. It was a *partnership* between me and my soul. I felt why I didn't want the experience of surrendering my Ego during the MDMA journey. I didn't want to float around in the abyss and the unknown during my time on earth. I would have eternity to live as a soul, as a spirit, but I had a limited time here on earth as human, as Natasha, and I wanted to experience all of it.

I lay there with Magic D. In that moment, I didn't feel burdened by my history or my trauma; instead, I felt such gratitude for the depth of the human experience I was gifted. In forty years, I had experienced pain, sorrow, suffering, grief, rage, power, powerlessness, helplessness, and service. All of it. I was the luckiest girl on the planet, truly the girl with a rosemary ham no longer searching for that scrap of bread. I also saw how the challenges of my life had prepared me for my purpose of teaching and helping others, a life of service and contribution. This life of service wasn't because it made me a good person, but because I chose to connect with others and support them through their pain and journeys back to wholeness. Back to wholeness, because it's there waiting for them if they'll stop searching outside themselves.

My mind shifted to my father, and I felt immense love for him as I saw images of us walking through the woods when I was a child, swimming together in a lake, painting rooms of the house together. Then came a flash of images of my mother and me, and with them the same tender feelings. I could see the incredible strength in my mother, her courage, and how she loved my children unconditionally and how hard she worked to have a relationship with me. I could feel how much my parents loved me; they loved me so much. Yes, their Egos took in damage and trauma and acted out in pain, hurting me and those around them, but at the core, there was love. I chose to focus on the love they gave me and have compassion for the pain they held that they discharged. I'm okay, I have healed, and I am safe. There is no need for blame. I thanked them silently in my heart and had the knowing that my wisdom, discernment, and self-love would not allow any of their own or anyone else's broken Egos to abuse me or my children.

I then saw that my children, my beautiful boys, their souls and Egos, are here to learn the same truth in whatever way they're going to. I will choose not to abuse them through the trauma of my Ego. I will choose love when I can by mastering myself and building trust in the partnership of Ego and the divine. I also accept they will experience the pain they need from the world for them to awaken to the truth of this human experience, this gift.

Finally, another message came from deep within: *"Crisis is a gift. It affords the opportunity for consciousness. Don't protect people from it because it will just prolong the inevitable."* With that statement, I felt more gratitude, then saw an image of Paul. I choked up and went silent, fully focusing on the message coming through my consciousness. I looked at Magic D, who was smiling patiently, eyes alight, and I knew these messages were gifts of clarity for him, too. I almost whispered the rest of the message. *"I'm grateful to my body for not letting me stay married, not just for me, but for Paul and the children. I would have kept going in the marriage and caused more destruction and pain for myself and others. Thank you, body, for your wisdom, for the opportunity to awaken. And, I'm grateful for Paul. I'm grateful for the role he played in the tug-of-war that pushed me to see all that lay within. All of it forced me to learn to trust that I would be held."* I got it. The Universe won't intervene. It will let you destroy yourself and it will love you in it, but it's your free will that chooses to do something different, that can choose the path of healing back to wholeness and love.

Natasha Senra-Pereira

Natasha Senra-Pereira is a Registered Social Worker (MSW, RSW) and Psychotherapist (RP) who is committed to a life of service and connection. Her own path of learning and experience has been driven by the newest research in neuroscience, bridging modern science with the ancient healing traditions of psychedelics and spiritual practices. Her experience includes work in Canada's largest mental health hospital and maintaining a private practice. Her career is devoted to supporting those ready to move through and out of their current circumstances and into more dynamic and vibrant lives. She has been specifically drawn to supporting those who walk the most challenging paths, working in forensics and complex trauma and on crisis teams. Natasha has degrees in psychology and a master's degree in social work. She has further advanced trainings in numerous modalities, including somatic psychotherapy, IFS, and EMDR. She lives in Toronto with her family, raising her magically adorable sons in the pulse of downtown city life.

Further Reading

Becoming Supernatural: How Common People Are Doing the Uncommon by Dr. Joe Dispenza

The Body Keeps the Score: Brain, Mind, and Body in the Healing of Trauma by Dr. Bessel van der Kolk

The Book of Awakening: Having the Life You Want by Being Present to the Life You Have by Mark Nepo

Getting Past Your Past: Take Control of Your Life with Self-Help Techniques from EMDR Therapy by Dr. Francine Shapiro

A Healing Space: Befriending Ourselves in Difficult Times by Matt Licata

Healing Trauma: A Pioneering Program for Restoring the Wisdom of Your Body by Dr. Peter Levine

How to Change Your Mind: What the New Science of Psychedelics Teaches Us About Consciousness, Dying, Addictions, Depression, and Transcendence by Michael Pollan

Many Minds, One Self: Evidence for a Radical Shift in Paradigm by Richard C. Schwartz, Robert R. Falconer

No Bad Parts: Healing Trauma and Restoring Wholeness with the Internal Family Systems Model by Dr. Richard Schwartz

The Science of the Art of Psychotherapy by Dr. Alan Schore

The Seat of the Soul by Gary Zukav

Soul Shaping: A Journey of Self-Creation by Jeff Brown

The Untethered Soul: The Journey Beyond Yourself
by Michael A. Singer

When the Body Says No: The Cost of Hidden Stress
by Dr. Gabor Maté

The Whole-Brain Child: 12 Revolutionary Strategies to Nurture Your Child's Developing Mind by Dr. Daniel Siegel
and Dr. Tina Bryson

Acknowledgments

There are many people to thank for their encouragement, expertise, and enthusiasm for this book. I must begin with Trevor—a man so rooted in himself he never needs to uproot me. Thank you for chopping wood and carrying water alongside me. And thank you for being the first to tell me that "the Universe is either nothing or everything."

To my kiddos—I love you, and I hope you'll invite me to be a part of your healing journey when it's time. To their father, thank you for creating these two beautiful humans with me. To my own father, mother, sister, and brother—we made it through, and I'm so thankful to be on the other side with you. There is no other family I would want to move through life with. I love you.

A special acknowledgment to my brother, who sees truth and speaks it clearly and passionately.

To Lisa Kottoor—I am so grateful you *knew* that we would be friends. Thank you for your wisdom and strength, and for sharing your light with me and the world.

To Liz Philips—every time I think of you, I am reminded of the benevolence of the Universe and how it will bring me all that I need. My deepest appreciation and gratitude for our talks and love for each other.

To Danny Stillitano, Wendy MacLellan, and Sarah MacMillan—many have come and gone, as they should have, but I am so grateful for our continued friendships and support over the years of my unfolding. Much love for your enduring presence and patience.

To my Ryzio community—thank you for sitting in our circles, for witnessing, and for being my caring other.

To Melanie Dignam—I followed you out of church and into the sunshine to walk straight to the Source many years ago. You are a healer in this world.

To Laura Jamer—you are a woman who inspires and delights me. Thank you for supporting my dives into the unknown and encouraging my next steps.

To Jennifer Phelps—your brilliance and creative intuition were instrumental in bringing this book to fruition; many thanks for your early belief in this book and me.

And to the incredible team at Modern Wisdom Press, including Catherine Gregory and Nathan Joblin—you have created a transformational process to assist authors in birthing their books. Thank you for midwifing me. And to Gabrielle Idlet, for her editing artistry and for feeling the heart of these words on the page.

I am limited in language when it comes to the gratitude and love I have for the mentors, healers, and teachers referenced in this book. These supernatural human beings led me back to myself with grace, humor, incredible skill, and gifts. Your humbleness and devotion to your clients and the work have transformed me—thank you for guiding me back to myself.

And to Dr. Bessel Van Der Kolk, Dr. Gabor Mate, and Dick Schwartz—sitting in your audience revolutionized my practice. Thank you for your courage in speaking a truth to the larger mental health field. Thank you.

Thank You

Some time ago, I was swimming in a lake when it began to rain. As the other swimmers headed to shore, I stayed, treading water, watching the slow smattering of drops pooling into the lake. It was slow, peaceful, and gentle. As I watched, I began to hear through my consciousness: *Each drop contributes to this larger body of water. Each drop is needed and has value. The quality of each drop informs the health of the lake.* In that moment, I understood my purpose, and I understood the work I wished to devote my life to.

I honor those who care for the lake, the collective, but my work is devoted to the quality and health of each drop. To every single client I have had the privilege of sitting with, my sincerest thanks for your devotion to your own healing and for trusting me to walk alongside you. Thank you for stepping into your wisdom and courage so that we can have a healthier collective—a community and an experience of peace and joy.

Many thanks from the seat of my soul and the fullness of my heart.

Next Steps

To my readers,

You may have learned that *talk therapy isn't enough* from your own experience of struggle and suffering. You are ready to move away from coping and managing and to step forward in creating a life of authenticity, enthusiasm, and joy. The first step is to breathe. This is not a *figure-it-out* path; this is a *follow-your-intuition* path.

I have dedicated my adult life to exploring and trying different therapy and healing modalities and understanding what works and why. From this knowledge and experience, I have created a series of programs and offerings that integrate the paradigms and evidence-based models that lead to true transformation. I invite you to explore what may resonate with you at www.TalkTherapyIsntEnough.com.

And, to paraphrase the wise Janice Hayes: Trust that you'll find your way, we all do it in our own time, and time is eternal.

—**Natasha Senra-Pereira**, MSW, RSW, RP

Made in the USA
Middletown, DE
28 June 2022